Contents

INTRODUCTION   4

WIRE 101   6

TOOLS AND SUPPLIES   9

ESSENTIAL TECHNIQUES   12

THE PROJECTS   31

Beginner

Janice's Pendant   32

Abby's Bracelet   36

Betty's Pendant   40

Trish's Necklace   44

Marie's Earrings   48

Intermediate

Misti's Bracelet   52

Christy's Earrings   56

Becky's Pendant   62

Lisa's Ring   66

Kathy's Bracelet   70

DeeDee's Bracelet   76

Joanna's Bracelet   82

Judy's Earrings   88

Isabella's Pendant   92

Denise's Earrings   96

Charli's Bracelet   100

Advanced

Victoria's Pendant   104

Jan's Cross   110

Jules' Bracelet   116

Michelle's Necklace   122

Franchezka's Necklace   128

ACKNOWLEDGMENTS   134

RESOURCES   134

INDEX   135

Introduction

Artisan Filigree

Wire-Wrapping Jewelry Techniques and Projects

Jodi Bombardier

INTERWEAVE.
interweave.com

To my #1 girl, Jules.
Thanks for all the notes of encouragement you left for me to find in my studio. You're the best.

Editor Michelle Bredeson

Technical Editor Jane Dickerson

Associate Art Director Julia Boyles

Cover & Interior Adrian Newman

Illustrator Bonnie Brooks

Photographer Joe Coca

Photo Stylist Ann Sabin Swanson

Production Katherine Jackson

© 2013 Jodi Bombardier

Photography and illustrations © 2013 Interweave Press LLC

All rights reserved.

Interweave Press LLC
A division of F+W Media, Inc.
201 East Fourth Street
Loveland, CO 80537
interweave.com

Manufactured in China by Asia Pacific Offset Ltd.

Library of Congress Cataloging-in-Publication Data

Bombardier, Jodi.
  Artisan filigree : wire-wrapping jewelry techniques and projects / Jodi Bombardier.

  Includes bibliographical references and index.
  ISBN 978-1-59668-635-9 (pbk.)
  ISBN 978-1-62033-115-6 (PDF)
  1. Jewelry making. 2. Wire jewelry. I. Title.
  TT212.B643 2013
  745.594'2--dc23

                    2012033942

10 9 8 7 6 5 4 3 2 1

I started making jewelry in 2001. After dabbling in memory wire, stringing, and chain maille, I discovered wire and never looked back! The ways to twist and bend wire seem endless, and seeing what other artisans create with wire provides constant fuel for my creativity.

For most of my wire jewelry designs, I draw inspiration from architecture. Living in the Southwest, I'm surrounded by wrought-iron fences and gates filled with scrolls. The magnificent swirls of vintage jewelry also give me ideas for wire designs.

In my research on filigree jewelry, I've found several definitions. Here is my interpretation: Filigree jewelry is made up of fine wires shaped into intricate patterns in open soldered designs or designs soldered to a metal base. Typically, gold or silver wire is used. In *Artisan Filigree,* the projects involve cold rather than hot (soldering) connections. The shapes are created in heavier-gauge wire, then coiled or woven together with finer-gauge wire, and sometimes connected with jump rings, to become pendants, bracelets, earrings, and rings. Changing the orientation of the shapes creates new designs, and, in some more complex projects, several different shapes are used in a single design. In my jewelry designs, I have long used frames that are woven, coiled, or embellished in some way, so *Artisan Filigree* felt like a natural progression. In a couple of projects in my first book, *Weave, Wrap, Coil,* such as Caesar's Scrolls Bracelet and Melonia's Cross, you can see the beginning of this direction.

As I developed designs for *Artisan Filigree,* I made countless shapes of varying sizes, with different wire gauges, using both square and round wire. I would spread the shapes out on my work bench and then start playing, fitting the shapes together in various orientations and sometimes placing stones in between the shapes to see what designs evolved. Sometimes, I would take a magnificent stone and see what shapes fit around it. One example of working shapes around a stone is Janice's Pendant (page 32). When I saw a strand of golden rutilated quartz at a bead show, I just had to have it and use it in a design!

I've worked with a variety of wire types and gauges over the years, including craft, copper, brass, sterling silver, and fine silver wire, with gauges ranging from 28 to 8. I use round, square, and half-round wire in my work. The designs in *Artisan Filigree* are created with craft, copper, and sterling silver wire in a mix of shapes and gauges. Please note: If a project is shown in sterling silver wire, for example, that doesn't mean that you have to use sterling silver. Have fun and use the wire type and shape of your choice! Although projects can be made with different gauges, I suggest you use the same gauge I use the first time you make a project.

The projects in this book are sorted into three categories: beginner, intermediate, and advanced. They incorporate wire-form shaping, coiling, weaving, wire wrapping, or a combination of techniques. The trick to many of these techniques is to understand how to work with your tools and how to manipulate your wire to get it to consistently do what you want it to do. See Skill Levels below to figure out which projects to try first.

So let's get the creativity going. Dig into the projects in *Artisan Filigree* and see what works of art you come up with. I hope you enjoy making the projects in my book and learn many new techniques!

Skill Levels

These descriptions of the projects in this book will help you decide which ones will best fit your level of jewelry-making experience.

Beginner

These projects are written to teach consistency in wire-form shaping and present a systematic way of connecting shapes together. Beginner projects are mostly made with one style of shape. Intermediate and advanced level designers will quickly grasp the construction of these pieces.

Intermediate

These projects are for someone who is comfortable with wire-form shaping, but who needs some guidance on systematically assembling the pieces. Intermediate projects include one or more shapes. If only one shape is used, the connections will be more complex than in a beginner-level project. The advanced designer may need to skim the instructions and illustrations of an intermediate project, but more than likely will be able to look at the project and understand its construction.

Advanced

These more challenging projects are for artists who are proficient with wire-form shaping, but who may need a little help understanding how the pieces are constructed.

Marie's Earrings, page 50

Wire 101

My secret is out—I LOVE WIRE. It's forgiving, it can be manipulated into just about any shape you can imagine, and it comes in a variety of materials, shapes, and gauges. I work primarily with sterling silver, copper, and craft wire. This chapter will get you started on the right path to making filigree jewelry with wire.

TYPES OF METAL

Wire comes in many different metals. For the projects in *Artisan Filigree*, I use the wires listed below. As you work through the projects in the book, remember that you can use any type of wire—copper, sterling silver, or craft—for any of the projects. (Some designers like to work with brass wire; because I find it too stiff and springy, I didn't use it in these projects.)

Copper Wire

I love copper wire. It's naturally dead-soft (see Wire Hardness, page 7) and the price is right! Keep in mind that bare copper wire can vary in color from one spool to the next. I discovered this while making a bracelet; I ran out of wire, started a new spool, and didn't notice the color difference until the bracelet was finished. You can easily ensure that this doesn't happen by using nontarnish natural-color copper wire, which has a clear coating.

Craft Wire

There are several brands of craft wire on the market. My favorite is ParaWire, a brand of non-tarnish copper wire that's coated with a color. (ParaWire also offers a natural-color copper wire that is nontarnish and a bare copper wire that can be oxidized.) The selection of colors is phenomenal. Though most of the projects in this book are shown in antique copper and vintage bronze, I used purple 18-gauge craft wire with copper 26-gauge wire for my first mock-up of Charli's Bracelet (page 100), to which my daughter Jules responded, "Awesome, Mom!" Craft wire gives you the opportunity to create some fun color combinations.

Sterling Silver Wire

Sterling silver wire is 92.5 percent silver and 7.5 percent copper. Sterling silver wire is quite a bit more expensive than copper or craft wire, and the copper component in sterling silver causes it to tarnish.

WIRE GAUGES

Wire comes in a wide range of gauges (diameters). On the American Standard Wire Gauge chart, the narrowest wire is 38-gauge and the widest is 1-gauge. In this book, I use gauges in the middle of the range, with 26-gauge being the smallest and 16-gauge being the largest. You might think the gauging system seems backward—intuitively, 16 would be smaller than 26—but the gauge correlates to the number of times the wire is pulled through holes in steel plates to achieve the desired diameter. Each time the wire gets pulled, it's drawn through a smaller hole. Theoretically, that means that 26-gauge wire is pulled through holes in steel plates twenty-six times.

Wire Gauges

ROUND	HALF-ROUND	SQUARE	
•	▴	■	16g
•	▴	■	18g
•	▴	■	19g
•	•	■	20g
•	•	■	21g
•	•	•	22g
•	•	•	24g
·	·	·	26g

WIRE SHAPES

If you look at the cross-section of a piece of wire, it will be round, square, or half-round. For projects in this book, I use all three shapes of wire. Which one I choose depends on the look I want and the technique I'm using. I sometimes mix round and square wire in the same piece. For Denise's Earrings (page 96), I use round wire for the pieces in the center and square wire for the earring frames. In Essential Techniques (page 12), I offer some pointers for using each shape of wire.

WIRE HARDNESS

Wire is available in different measures of hardness: dead-soft, half-hard, and hard. Dead-soft wire is very malleable and easy to work with. Half-hard wire has some stiffness to it but isn't as stiff as hard wire.

All wire has a "spring-back" to it. For example, when you're making a coil to cut jump rings, the coil will loosen somewhat, or spring back, when you stop coiling the wire. The harder the wire, the more spring-back it has, with dead-soft wire having the least spring-back.

I use dead-soft wire for coiling and weaving. It's easier to shape and bend when you make loops and arches. For such purposes, it's important to have flexibility in the wire, because it's easier to manipulate. With less spring-back, it's easier to accomplish the shapes you strive to make. Even dead-soft wire is stiffer in larger gauges, however, because of its thick diameter.

In my experience, the tails of half-hard wire curl and must be constantly straightened to avoid kinking, especially with 26-gauge wire. The tails of dead-soft wire won't curl as much,

and they can be straightened. I do use half-hard wire for ear wires because it helps them hold their shape through repeated wearing. I don't use hard wire.

The metal the wire is made of affects its hardness. Dead-soft sterling silver is a bit stiffer than copper wire, and colored craft wire can be stiffer than silver or copper because of the color coating. Fine-silver wire is extremely soft and costs more than sterling; although I haven't tested it, I believe it wouldn't hold a shape well.

Ultimately, the decision whether to use dead-soft or half-hard wire depends on personal preference. Experiment and see what works best for you!

Which Wire Should You Use?

With each project, the instructions indicate the gauge and length of wire needed and the shape of wire I used. Feel free to use a different metal than what I use. If I use sterling silver, for example, you can easily substitute copper wire. If you change the gauge, however, the measurements might change. They might also change if you switch from round to square wire or vice versa, because square wire takes up more space than round wire. How much the measurements will change depends on the shape being made and how the shapes are positioned within or next to each other.

Cost Considerations

In addition to aesthetics and the characteristics of the wire, you'll want to consider the final cost of the jewelry piece you're making before you decide which type of wire to use. I always use copper and craft wire for making mock-ups and creating new designs. I also use copper and craft wire in many finished projects because I can't resist the beauty of copper or the variety of color. For a labor-intensive piece, I sometimes use sterling silver. When I finished my second mock-up of Charli's Bracelet (page 100), my husband asked me how much I could sell the bracelet for. I explained that a piece that takes a few hours to make is, in my opinion, better made with sterling silver so my time is justified in the price of the piece. In the buyer's eye, the same piece made with craft or copper wire would not be perceived as having the same value as one made with sterling silver, even if it took just as long to make.

Misti's Bracelet, page 52

SAFETY

The first rule in working with wire is to be safe. Wire can be sharp so use common sense! Cutting wire creates a sharp edge, and pieces of wire can become flying missiles as you cut. Cup your hand over the wire as you cut it to keep a wire piece from flying across the room or into your eye.

STRAIGHTENING WIRE

Wire is typically sold in a coil or on a spool. You'll want to straighten it before you work with it. Straighten the wire with nylon-jaw wire-straightening pliers or by pulling it through a folded cleaning pad or cloth.

CLEANLINESS

Like me, you might automatically apply lotion after washing your hands. It's not a great idea if you're going to work with wire. Lotion will dirty the wire and make it difficult to hold on to. Because even natural body oils can make wire dirty, it's smart to wash your hands before working with wire (and skip the lotion!). If the wire does get dirty, you can clean it with a disposable polishing pad or cloth available at jewelry supply stores and in retail jewelry stores.

STORAGE

I like to store my wire in plastic bags. It keeps the dust off the wire and can cut down on tarnish. I write the wire gauge and shape right on the plastic bag and keep the bags in a plastic multidrawer container with wheels, so I can move it to wherever I'm working.

You should also store each piece of finished wire jewelry in a plastic bag to protect it from dust and to slow tarnishing. You can tumble the jewelry in this book to polish it, but if you don't have a tumbler, you can use a jewelry polishing pad or cloth. Take care when you wipe the wire on the back of a piece because the polishing pad may snag on the coiled or woven wire ends.

RECYCLING WIRE SCRAPS

Sterling silver wire can be recycled through refiners. I store my scrap in a plastic container (I never store the wire scrap in a plastic baggie because the wire ends can poke through) and take it to a refiner who will give me cash for it. Look for refiners online.

Wire artisan Maria Richmond of Lost Marbles works only with copper wire. She tells me that copper wire scrap can be recycled at a scrap yard, not through a refiner. Because copper wire is inexpensive to purchase and the payback is low, you'll want to save up a few pounds of scrap before taking it to your local scrap yard.

Tools and Supplies

The projects in this book require commonly used wire-working tools. Although it's wonderful to have a big stash of unusual tools, you can go far with a few good-quality basics. Here are the tools I recommend to make the projects in *Artisan Filigree*.

FLUSH CUTTERS

A sharp pair of flush cutters *(figure 1)* is essential to getting clean cuts on wire. Flush cutters have a flat side and a concave side. Always hold the flat side of the cutters against your work and the concave side against the waste. The flat side creates a nice flush, or flat, cut on one end of the wire, while the concave side creates a pinched (slightly pointed) cut on the other side of the wire. You'll sometimes want to make a second flush cut on the pinched side (for example, when you make jump rings), so both ends are flat and level. For the projects in this book, you'll be using flush cuts.

CHAIN-NOSE AND FLAT-NOSE PLIERS

Chain-nose *(figure 2)* and flat-nose pliers are used to hold wire and jewelry pieces and to bend wire. Chain-nose pliers taper to a point, while flat-nose pliers are straight and square at the tip. Chain-nose pliers are ideal when you need to pull coiling and weaving wire through small spaces. Although chain-nose pliers can be used to bend wire, flat-nose pliers create a sharper, crisper bend.

ROUND-NOSE PLIERS

Round-nose pliers *(figure 3)* come in a variety of barrel sizes and are used to make loops and jump rings. Most projects in this book require a small loop, which you can make with the narrow end of medium round-nose pliers, but a few call for large-diameter loops (up to 7 mm), so you may need more than one size. To make multiple loops of the same size, you'll need to mark the pliers with a permanent marker. (I explain how to do this on page 14 of Essential Techniques).

BAIL-MAKING PLIERS

Although not absolutely essential for completing the projects in this book, bail-making pliers *(figure 4)* are quite handy! Unlike round-nose pliers, the barrels of bail-making pliers aren't tapered, so they don't "tilt" square wire as round-nose pliers do. Each barrel of bail-making pliers is a different size. I have three pairs (made by Wubbers) in my toolbox, with these size barrels: 2/2.5mm, 3/5mm, and 7/9mm. Bail-making pliers ensure that the same size loop is made time and again, and they eliminate the need to measure and mark round-nose pliers with a permanent marker, which wears off easily. I also use bail-making pliers to make coils to cut into jump rings.

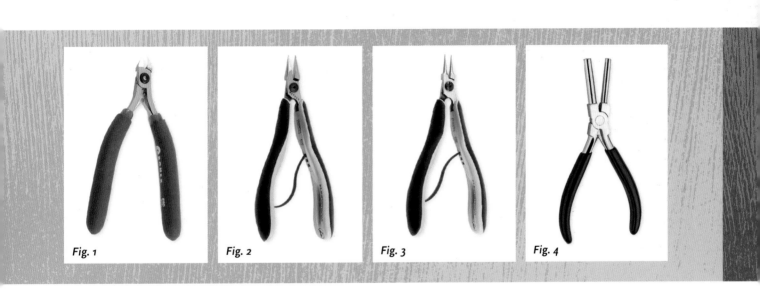

Fig. 1   *Fig. 2*   *Fig. 3*   *Fig. 4*

NYLON-JAW WIRE-STRAIGHTENING PLIERS

Nylon-jaw wire-straightening pliers *(figure 5)* do just that—straighten out crooked wire. To straighten wire, bend *into* the crooked or bent part, overextending the wire in that same direction, then pull the wire through the pliers a few times to straighten it. I used to think that I should bend *against* the crooked part I was trying to straighten out—wrong! Doing so makes the kink in the wire worse. To avoid leaving tool marks, I also use my nylon-jaw wire-straightening pliers (rather than chain- or flat-nose pliers) to open and close loops and jump rings. Nylon on metal is slippery, though, so it's not always possible to use wire-straightening nylon-jaw pliers if you're working in a really tight space.

NYLON-JAW BRACELET-FORMING PLIERS AND BRACELET MANDREL

Nylon-jaw bracelet-forming pliers are one of my favorite specialized tools. To use the pliers, gently squeeze the bracelet, starting at one end and working your way to the other. These pliers will create a gentle curve in the bracelet. A bracelet mandrel is likewise a handy shaping tool. With bracelets that tend to be springy, such as Charli's Bracelet (page 100), I start with nylon-jaw bracelet-forming pliers, then hook the bracelet around a mandrel as tightly as I can and press the individual filigree pieces against the mandrel to help shape and bend them.

MANDRELS

Mandrels are objects around which you can shape wire and forms to specific sizes. They are integral to the projects in this book, but you don't need to buy a variety of special mandrels. I recommend having a ring mandrel *(figure 6)*. Be sure to purchase a ring mandrel that isn't grooved because the groove can leave bend marks in the wire. Round-nose or bail-making pliers make great mandrels because the second jaw can be used to grasp the wire and hold it steady.

PERMANENT MARKER

Every toolbox needs a permanent marker for measuring and marking wire. These marks are usually covered with wire, during either coiling or weaving, but in some cases the mark will be partially exposed. To avoid visible marks in your finished jewelry, rub the marks off with a soft cotton cloth or disposable jewelry polishing cloth when they're no longer needed.

LOW-STICK TAPE

A roll of low-stick tape (blue painter's tape) is essential. You'll often be working with several small wire frames at one time, and this tape will be your best friend! Taping the wire frames together makes coiling and weaving much easier, and it takes the guesswork out of which frame goes next to which. Low-stick tape is available in hardware stores.

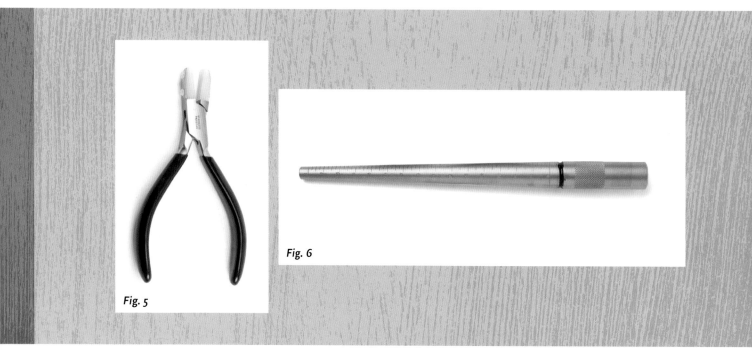

Fig. 5

Fig. 6

POLISHING CLOTH

A polishing cloth can be used to polish your wire and to remove marks made with a permanent marker. If my wire isn't too crooked or kinked when I pull it from a coil or spool, I use a polishing cloth to not only clean my wire but also gently straighten it. Polishing cloths are treated with a chemical, and as metal is cleaned and the chemical used up, the cloth turns from white to grayish-black.

METAL FILE

As you're coiling and weaving wire, you may feel sharp edges on the wire ends. Try to press a wire end into a space between the shapes or press it completely flat against a shape. Doing so usually eliminates the sharp edges. However, if you can't hide the wire ends, you can file them smooth. I find that a small flat pointed metal file works best for this. You can buy files in various sizes *(figure 7)* from a jewelry supply store.

SILVER BLACK AND LIVER OF SULFUR (LOS)

Silver Black is a liquid product that oxidizes silver and other metals and darkens it to enhance details or create a patina, or antique, effect. Liver of sulfur (LOS) is another chemical that will also patina silver and copper. I prefer Silver Black because its odor is milder than LOS's strong sulfur (rotten egg) smell. See Oxidizing Wire on page 30 for more discussion of how to use Silver Black and LOS.

TONGS OR TWEEZERS

Because Silver Black and LOS are active chemicals, you'll need tongs or tweezers to place wire or finished jewelry into and take it out of either liquid.

STEEL WOOL

After you've dipped wire into Silver Black or LOS, clean and polish it with 0000 steel wool for a satin finish. The more you rub the wire with steel wool, the more Silver Black or LOS will be removed. Go slowly to make sure you don't go too far!

ROTARY TUMBLER

Although not essential, a tumbler *(figure 8)* is a handy piece of equipment for quickly shining or cleaning jewelry. I use stainless steel shot and a small amount of burnishing liquid or Dawn brand dish soap as a degreaser. If you use a tumbler, watch carefully to make sure your jewelry doesn't get shinier than you want.

GRIDDED COMPOSITION PAPER

Some projects, such as Jan's Cross (page 110), require the wire pieces to be at a precise angle or perfectly straight. The squares on gridded composition paper, also called graph paper, are helpful for accuracy and precision. I use paper with a ¼" (6.4 mm) grid (4 squares = 1" [2.5 cm]). You can lay the pieces directly on the paper to check the angles. Gridded paper is also a useful tool for sketching ideas to scale.

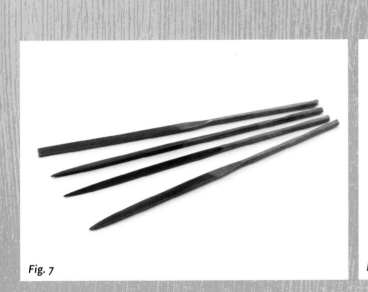

Fig. 7

Fig. 8

Essential Techniques

As you work through the projects in this book, you'll be referred back to this section for techniques such as creating shapes and making jump rings. If any techniques are new to you, practice first before diving into a project. Even if you're an old hand at jewelry making, you may want to read through and possibly practice my methods. I may do something in a new way that could inspire you!

Essential Organizational Tips

Here are a few practices I've developed over the years to help me stay organized when making filigree jewelry:

Bag and Label Practice Pieces
I think you'll find them handy as a point of reference when you make projects from this book or design your own filigree pieces.

Take Meticulous Notes
I do this for everything I make, so that if I want to remake a piece, I don't have to rethink the project. In my notes, I include wire gauge, size of loops, length of wire—anything that pertains to the piece I'm constructing.

Sketch on Graph Paper
I use gridded composition paper, or graph paper, with ¼" (6.4 mm) squares (4 squares = 1" [2.5 cm]) to sketch projects to scale and to check that wire components are straight when necessary, as with the L-shaped pieces in Jan's Cross (page 110).

BODY MECHANICS

How you manipulate the tools and where you hold the wire are important factors in the outcome of the loops and bends that you make. It's all about controlling your wire and letting the tools do the work for you.

Hand Position

Grasp the pliers in your dominant hand (for example, your right hand if you're right-handed) and hold the wire in your nondominant hand (your left hand). The closer to the tool you place the hand holding the wire (the nondominant hand), the greater control you'll have over the wire.

Hold for Wire Stability and Control

To have complete control over the wire when you use a tool, hold the wire with your nondominant hand right next to the tool, with your fingers touching the tool. Holding the wire in this manner keeps the wire stable for consistent size and shape in your loops and clean, sharp bends.

Hold for Wire Flexibility

If you want the wire to be flexible as you use a tool, hold the wire with your nondominant hand away from the tool. I choose this method when I make Arched Loops (page 16).

Work Left to Right

We read and write from left to right and it makes sense to me to coil and weave from left to right. For the projects in this book, the instructions are written to guide you to coil and weave in this direction.

Roll Pliers Away from You

I learned wire wrapping from Mark Lareau's book *All Wired Up* (Interweave, 2000). Lareau instructs the reader to roll or bend the pliers away from the body, and this is what I've always done. There are exceptions to this rule, but it's important to develop a consistent construction style and use the exceptions only when necessary.

Let the Tools Do the Work

I often see students pulling the wire around the tool rather than rolling or bending the tool against the wire. Pulling the wire around the tool allows too much flexibility in the wire, creating inconsistency in the results. If you can't roll or bend your tool, or if the step you are trying to achieve requires pushing—not pulling—the wire around a tool, it's best to start pushing at the point where the wire touches the tool and work your way around the tool. If the wire ends need to cross over each other, you can continue pushing the wire against the tool.

BASIC WIRE-WORKING TECHNIQUES

Before we get into creating specific shapes, let's go over a few best practices for working with wire. The projects in this book are made with 26-, 22-, 21-, 20-, 18-, and 16-gauge dead-soft half-round, round, and square wire. I suggest practicing the techniques that follow with 18-gauge wire.

Matching Pliers to Wire

When making loops in square wire, it's best to use bail-making pliers, because the wire won't "tilt" on the straight jaws. If you don't have bail-making pliers, you can use round-nose pliers. The tapered jaws will cause the wire to tilt, but it can be straightened (see Making Loops in Square Wire on page 15). Use only flat-nose pliers to bend square wire, because chain-nose pliers, which have tapered jaws, will tilt the wire, and it can't be straightened.

Aligning Wire Shapes

Square wire, rather than round wire, is my first choice for the projects in this book. When square wire is coiled together, the wire shapes sit neatly next to each other. With round wire, one wire can ride up onto the second wire to which it's being coiled.

To successfully align round-wire shapes that have been coiled, use nylon-jaw wire-straightening pliers and gently squeeze over the coil. Although one wire can still slip up onto the other, this technique should align the two shapes side by side. Even with square wire, one shape may sit higher than the second shape because of pulling on the coiling wire. A gentle squeeze with nylon-jaw wire-straightening pliers should fix this problem. The riding-up effect doesn't occur when you weave with either square or round wire.

Loop Sizes

To achieve beautiful finished jewelry, pieces of filigree must fit together, and the key is to make consistently sized loops for each project. For this reason, I prefer to use bail-making pliers—my loops are then always the same size and I don't have to worry about constantly re-marking my round-nose pliers with a permanent marker. A project may include different size loops for different components, but loops that are intended to be the same size must be so. For example, Marie's Earrings (page 48) have 3 mm loops for the outer Heart shapes and 2 mm loops for the smaller Heart shapes. If the loop sizes are not exact, the Heart shapes won't fit together perfectly and the earrings won't match!

Judy's Earrings, page 88

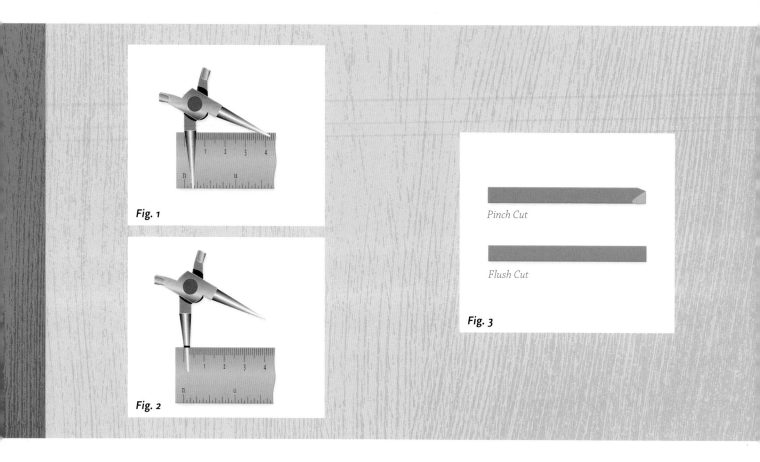

Fig. 1

Fig. 2

Pinch Cut

Flush Cut

Fig. 3

Measuring and Marking Round-Nose Pliers and Mandrels

The instructions for each project in this book indicate the size of the loops I made. If you use bail-making pliers, you'll be able to get the exact same measurements. If you want to duplicate these projects without using bail-making pliers, you must measure and mark the diameter of your round-nose pliers. The diameter of round-nose pliers can be measured with a caliper. If you don't own a caliper, you can easily measure the diameter without one. Gather a pair of round-nose pliers, a ruler with metric measurements, and a permanent marker.

1. Begin by measuring the widest point of the barrel. Open the handles and place one barrel on the metric side of a ruler and measure. The diameter of the barrel in *figure 1* is 5 mm.

2. Move the pliers to measure the center of the barrel. The diameter of the center of the barrel shown in *figure 2* is 3 mm.

3. Continue to move the barrel up or down on the ruler until you arrive at the measurement for the size loops desired. Mark the pliers with a permanent marker. Keep the marker handy, because the mark will wear off with every few loops you make. (Save time by re-marking your pliers before the mark wears off completely.)

Flush Cut and Pinch Cut

Flush cutters create what's called a pinch cut with the concave side of the jaws and a flat, or flush, cut with the flat side of the jaws *(figure 3)*. Always hold the flat side of the cutters against your work and the concave side against the waste. Be sure to use a flush cut for the techniques and projects in this book, except with 26-gauge wire, which is so fine that a flush cut isn't necessary. Practice flush-cutting the wire when you work with the techniques that follow.

MAKING LOOPS

I use a variety of loops in the projects in *Artisan Filigree*. Practice making all of them so you'll be ready when you need them.

P-Shaped Loop

The P-shaped Loop (so called because it looks like the letter P!) is the most basic loop. I used this loop in Betty's Pendant (page 40). You'll often need to know how much wire it takes to make a loop. As you follow the steps below to make a P-shaped Loop, you'll also learn how to determine the length of wire needed. To practice, straighten and flush-cut a 3" (7.6 cm) length of 18-gauge wire.

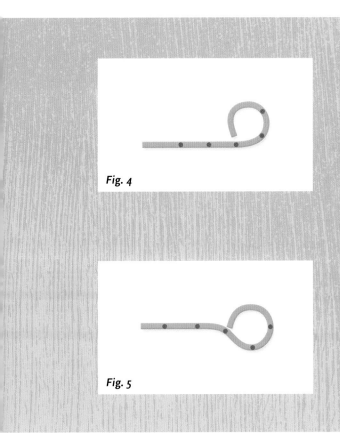

Fig. 4

Fig. 5

Making Loops in Square Wire

If you're using round-nose pliers to make loops in square wire, the wire will tilt to one side as you make the loops. The wire-straightening method that follows is an exception to the rule of always rolling away from you. Grasp one end of the wire with round-nose pliers. Make half a loop, rolling away from your body. Here's where things get different: turn the wire in the pliers, again ensuring that the wire tip can't be felt or can just barely be felt in the jaws of the pliers. Then, make the second half of the loop, rolling toward your body so you can watch the wire as you roll, ensuring that it's straightening.

1. With a permanent marker, mark the wire every ⅛" (3.2 mm), starting at ¼" (6.4 mm) and marking through ¾" (1.9 cm).

2. With bail-making pliers or round-nose pliers, grasp the wire end (if using round-nose pliers, grasp the wire on the 3 mm measurement mark). The tip of the wire should be as flush as possible to the jaws of the pliers so that when you run your finger along the jaws, you don't feel the wire at all or just barely feel it. If the wire tip sticks beyond the jaws of the pliers, the wire sticking out will be flattened and the loop will be oval in shape. Adjust the wire in the jaws if necessary.

3. Roll the pliers away from you about one-quarter turn or until your wrist is fully extended in a rolling motion. Reposition the pliers in the loop, being sure to turn the wire if you're using round-nose pliers on square wire, and finish rolling the wire until the flush-cut end touches the wire. Looking at the measurement mark of where the wire touches tells me that I used ½" (1.3 cm) of wire to make a 3 mm P-shaped Loop *(figure 4)*. The length of wire used for the loops will change with each wire gauge and size of bail-making or round-nose pliers that you use.

Simple Loop

The Simple Loop is slightly different from the P-shaped Loop in that it has a neck. In other words, the Simple Loop is centered over the straight part of the wire like a lollipop

For practice, straighten and flush-cut 3" (7.6 cm) of 18-gauge dead-soft wire. Use 3mm bail-making pliers or round-nose pliers measured and marked at 3 mm.

Follow the steps for the P-shaped Loop. To turn a P-shaped Loop into a Simple Loop, use chain-nose pliers and grab the wire just inside the loop. With wire control (see page 12), bend the wire to center the loop over the neck. The loop may open up a bit when you center it. If it does, use bail-making or round-nose pliers to roll the loop until it touches the wire again *(figure 5)*.

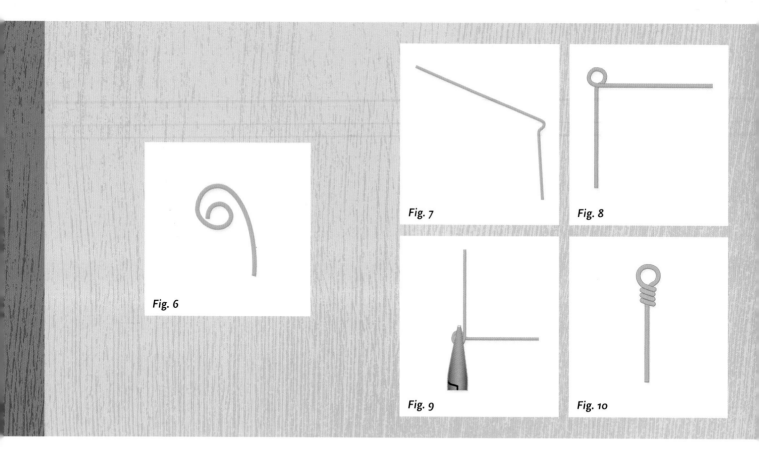

Fig. 6

Fig. 7

Fig. 8

Fig. 9

Fig. 10

Arched Loop

The Arched Loop is an extension of a P-shaped Loop. It creates a pretty arch that's used in Isabella's Pendant (page 92) and Marie's Earrings (page 48). The Arched Loop is a freeform style, and it can be made in different sizes and angles. For practice, straighten and flush-cut 3" (7.6 cm) of 18-gauge dead-soft wire.

1. With bail-making pliers or round-nose pliers, follow the instructions for a P-shaped Loop (page 14), making a loop on one end of the wire.

2. Grasp the wire with the loop facing away from you and, with wire flexibility (see page 12), slowly roll the loop away from you to create an arch in the wire *(figure 6)*.

   Note: *Because the Arched Loop is freeform, the size of the arch depends on what you need it for. In the case of ear wires, it will need to be larger and more open than the Arched Loops used for other purposes.*

When you use Arched Loops for a project, the arches can be adjusted by rolling the loops more or less, according to how your pieces fit together. It's not a good idea to unroll an arch because you can lose part of it, creating a flat area. It's best to under-roll slightly so that you have room to roll more, if necessary, to make the pieces uniform in size and ensure that they fit together. The loops can also be pulled up or down to change the location of the loop in relation to the arch.

Wrapped Loop

The Wrapped Loop is similar to the Simple Loop, but the neck is coiled so the loop can't pull open, making it more secure than a Simple Loop. In a few projects, such as Janice's Pendant (page 32), I made Wrapped Loops with head pins to create a bead dangle. It's easiest to make Wrapped Loops with 18-gauge, or thinner, wire. It's certainly possible to make them with 16-gauge or larger wire, but it's more difficult to do so. For practice, cut 6" (15.2 cm) of 18-gauge dead-soft wire.

1. With flat-nose pliers, form a 90-degree bend 2" (5.1 cm) from one end of the wire. If you are making a wrapped loop on a head pin with a bead, grasp the wire about ⅛" (3.2 mm) above the bead, leaving room for coiling (See Step 5).

2. Grab the wire with the small to middle section of the round-nose pliers, then with wire control (see page 12), roll the pliers away from you until about one-half of the loop is made, but stop before the bend is rolled out *(figure 7)*. The idea is to center the loop over the bend.

3. While holding the wire in the pliers, grab the wire tail with your nondominant hand and pull it underneath the pliers so it's perpendicular to the wire stem. As you pull the wire, you may need to roll your pliers again slightly to avoid over- or under-extending the loop. Watch to make sure you don't roll or pull the bend out *(figure 8)*.

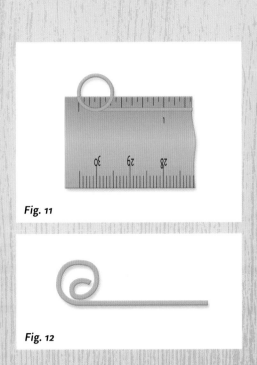

Fig. 11

Fig. 12

Changing Sizes

You'll find specific lengths and measurements in the instructions in this book. If you want a pendant larger or smaller than the wire measurements you see, cut shorter or longer pieces of wire, being sure to subtract or add in the same increment to each piece of wire used for the project. For example, if you add in ¼" (6.4 mm) on one piece of wire, you must add ¼" (6.4 mm) to every piece of wire. If you want larger loops, just be consistent about those as well. Practice with craft wire! Have fun and get those creative ideas flowing! Just remember, it's all about keeping everything symmetrical.

4. Use chain-nose pliers to grasp the loop just made with the wire tail facing away from you *(figure 9)*.

5. With your nondominant hand, grab the wire tail and coil it around the wire stem three or four times, then flush-cut the wire tail *(figure 10)*.

Regal Loop

This is a cool technique that creates over-rolled loops identical in size. DeeDee's Bracelet (page 76) and Denise's Earrings (page 96) use this technique. When you use this technique in a project, the instructions indicate which size bail-making or round-nose pliers to use. For practice, use 7mm and 2mm bail-making or round-nose pliers, and straighten and flush-cut 3" (7.6 cm) of 18-gauge dead-soft wire.

1. With 7mm bail-making pliers or round-nose pliers, loop one wire end, over-rolling the loop by ¼" (6.4 mm). Lay the wire flat on a ruler and measure from the wire end where the loop begins to the point where the loop intersects with the straight section of the wire *(figure 11)*.

2. Open the loop by pulling it out parallel to the wire base. With 2mm bail-making pliers or round-nose pliers, make a loop on the wire end.

3. Close the loop. The large loop should be touching the wire. If it isn't, grab the small loop with bail-making pliers or round-nose pliers and gently pull it down or roll the 7 mm loop slightly in and down until it touches.

   Note: *When you make smaller loops, such as 5 mm and 2 mm loops, the 5 mm loop may sit on top of the wire when the loop is closed. If this happens, gently pull the loop open until it rests alongside the wire **(figure 12)**.*

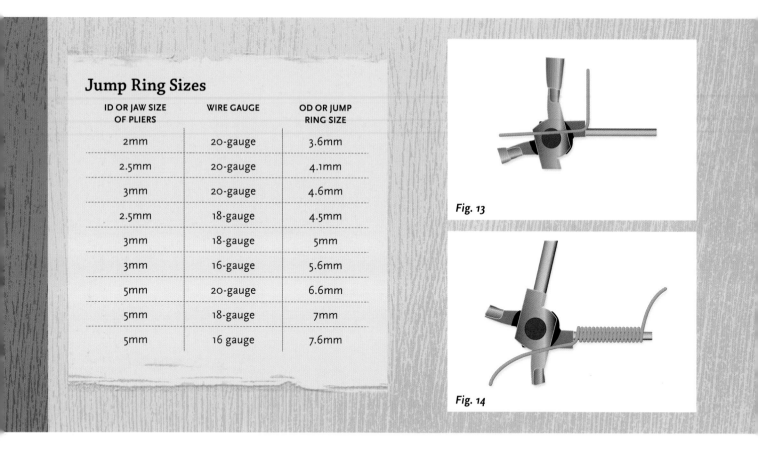

Jump Ring Sizes

ID OR JAW SIZE OF PLIERS	WIRE GAUGE	OD OR JUMP RING SIZE
2mm	20-gauge	3.6mm
2.5mm	20-gauge	4.1mm
3mm	20-gauge	4.6mm
2.5mm	18-gauge	4.5mm
3mm	18-gauge	5mm
3mm	16-gauge	5.6mm
5mm	20-gauge	6.6mm
5mm	18-gauge	7mm
5mm	16 gauge	7.6mm

Fig. 13

Fig. 14

JUMP RINGS

A jump ring is a small wire circle or oval used to link elements of a project. I always make circular jump rings and use round wire in a size proportionate to the project to which the rings are being attached. For example, for Marie's Earrings (page 48), I used 20-gauge wire to make 4mm jump rings. A larger jump ring would have made the earrings look top-heavy and out of proportion. The 4mm size gives a flow to the overall appearance of the earring. See each project's materials list for the size of jump rings that I recommend.

I usually use 20-, 18-, or 16-gauge wire for jump rings, depending on the function of the jump rings or the look I want to achieve. I use 20-gauge wire when the strength of the wire isn't an issue, such as connecting a Cloverleaf to the top of an earring or joining chains together as in Marie's Earrings (page 48). I use 18- or 16-gauge wire where more strength is needed or where I may be pulling on the jump ring, such as at the end of a bracelet or necklace. For Betty's Pendant (page 40), I used 16-gauge wire for the jump rings and in the chain.

To make several jump rings, you create a coil, which is then cut into rings. Begin by cutting 12" (30.5 cm) of wire. The wire doesn't have to be flush-cut for making the coil. A coil can be made with bail-making or round-nose pliers, but using round-nose pliers makes it more challenging to keep the size of the coil consistent; the wire has to be grasped with the tool

and rolled, which can leave tool marks. Two sets of instructions follow. The first uses bail-making pliers and the second uses round-nose pliers.

When you purchase jump rings, the size of the ring pertains to the outside diameter (OD) of the ring. When you make jump rings, the inside diameter (ID) is the jaw size of the pliers. For example, if I want to make 4mm 20-gauge jump rings, I would use my 2.5mm bail-making pliers. In the materials list for each project, I indicate the OD. If you make your own jump rings, refer to the table below to know which size pliers to use. If you can't find the exact size jump ring in the table, choose the measurement that is closest.

Making Jump Rings with Bail-Making Pliers

1. With chain-nose pliers, make a bend 1" (2.5 cm) from the wire end, creating a tail to hold on to.

2. Open the jaws of bail-making pliers.

3. Hold the wire tail against the pliers' box so the wire is at a 90-degree angle to the jaws (*figure 13*).

4. Coil the wire around one jaw of the pliers (*figure 14*).

5. Remove the coil from the pliers. (See page 19 for cutting instructions.)

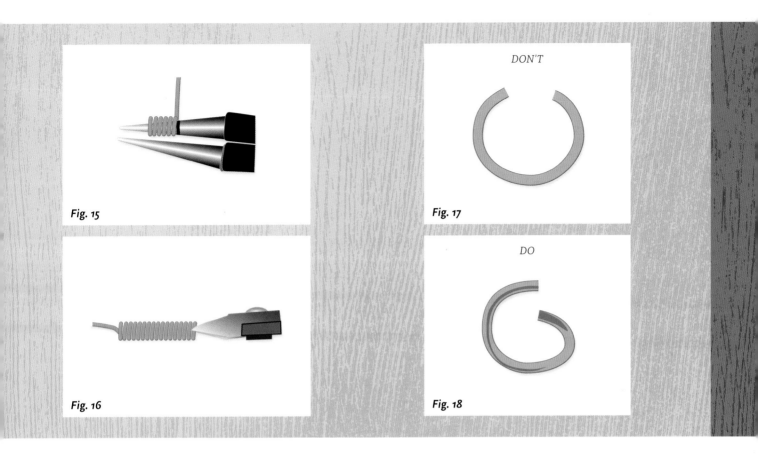

Fig. 15

Fig. 16

Fig. 17
DON'T

Fig. 18
DO

Making Jump Rings with Round-Nose Pliers

1. Measure and mark round-nose pliers at the size desired for your jump rings (see page 14). (You don't need to first make a bend in the wire as you do when you use bail-making pliers.)

2. Grasp the end of the wire on the mark, then roll the wire in the pliers, rolling the wire end toward the tip of the pliers. Continue rolling the wire around the pliers, keeping the wire on the permanent marker spot to create a uniform coil *(figure 15)*.

Cutting Jump Rings

After you create the coil, you cut the coil into individual jump rings.

1. For ease of cutting, slightly separate the coil by pulling the wire tails. Flush-cut one of the wire tails, then flush-cut the coil next to the end of the wire *(figure 16)*.

2. Flush-cut the pinch cut from the end of the coil, then flush-cut the coil next to the end of the wire. Continue cutting the coil until all jump rings have been cut.

Opening and Closing Jump Rings

Sometimes you need to open a loop to coil within the loop. Never uncurl the loop *(figure 17)*, because it will lose its shape. To open and close jump rings, grasp the ring on each side of the opening with nylon-jaw wire-straightening or chain-nose pliers pliers. Gently push one side away from you while pulling the other side toward you, so the ring opens from side to side *(figure 18)*. To close, reverse the direction of your hands. Do not pull the ends out to the side to open; this will weaken the jump ring.

Mass Production

Because I think it's a pain to make two jump rings here, four jump rings there, etc., I always make a coil, cut the number of rings needed, then store the remainder of the coil in a baggie that I label with the coil ID, jump-ring OD, and the wire gauge used.

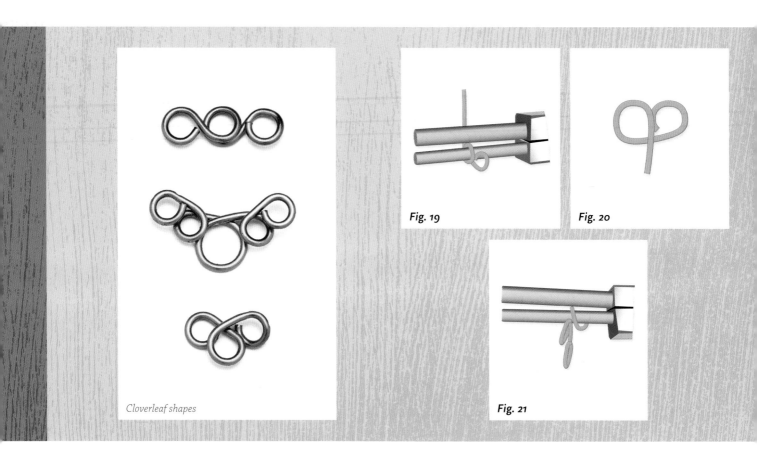

Cloverleaf shapes

Fig. 19

Fig. 20

Fig. 21

ESSENTIAL SHAPES

One of my goals in writing *Artisan Filigree* is to show that simple wire shapes can be oriented and combined into myriad pieces of eye-catching jewelry. In this section, you'll learn to make some of my favorite shapes. Each can be made in a variety of sizes. Some projects include additional shapes that are exclusive to those projects, with instructions included therein.

For each project, I recommend making all the shapes before starting to coil or weave the pieces together. Many shapes are duplicated within a design and should be made the same size or as close as possible to the same size, and you'll find it easier to compare shapes to each other when they're still loose. For consistency, I make one shape or cluster of shapes as a template and compare the remaining shapes or clusters to it.

To practice making these shapes, use 18- or 16-gauge round or square wire and make a loop size of your choice.

Cloverleaf

I love the look of the Cloverleaf. It offers a wide range of possibilities and adds a nice touch to any piece of jewelry. I make the loop sizes to fit the size of the jewelry I'm creating.

The Cloverleaf shape can be made with 20-, 18-, or 16-gauge round or square wire. If you're using round-nose pliers with square wire, remember to turn your wire halfway through each loop so your wire doesn't tilt. I like to make my outside loops smaller than my middle loops. If you're using round-nose

pliers, be sure to mark the pliers' jaws with a permanent marker so you make consistently sized loops.

Note: *I make the Cloverleaf directly from a wire spool or coil (of dead-soft wire) rather than first cutting a piece of wire. Doing so cuts down on wire waste and it's easier to hold on to the Cloverleaf while it's being made. Below, I describe how to make three variations of a Cloverleaf.*

Three-Loop Cloverleaf

1. Working from a spool or coil of 18-gauge wire, flush-cut the end of the wire. With bail-making or round-nose pliers, make a loop on the wire end. This is an outside loop.

2. Using larger diameter bail-making pliers or moving the wire to a larger diameter on your round-nose pliers, grab the wire next to the loop made in Step 1 to make the middle loop. As you make the loop, guide the wire so that it loops around the pliers to the left of the loop made in Step 1, rolling the wire around until a complete loop is formed **(figures 19 and 20)**.

3. Using the same diameter bail-making pliers or same smaller diameter on your round-nose pliers as in Step 1, grab the wire next to the middle loop and make the second outside loop. As you make the loop, guide the wire so that it loops around the pliers to the right of the loop made in Step 2 **(figure 21)**.

4. Flush-cut the wire.

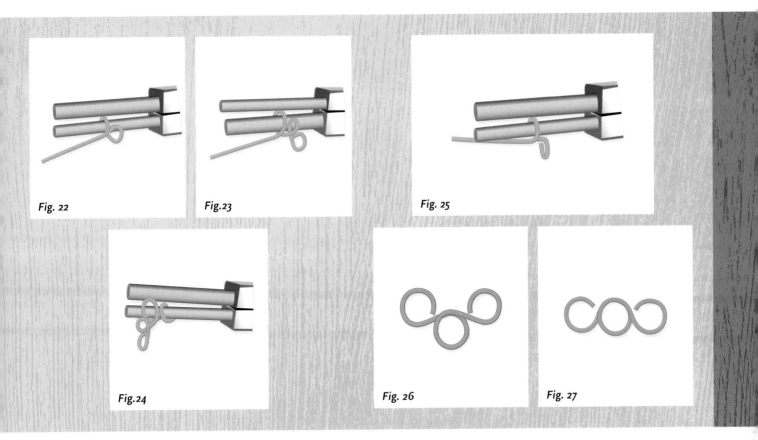

Fig. 22

Fig. 23

Fig. 25

Fig. 24

Fig. 26

Fig. 27

Five-Loop Cloverleaf

This Cloverleaf is made similarly to a Three-Loop Cloverleaf, with a pair of same-sized loops on either side of the central loop.

1. Working from a spool or coil of 18-gauge wire, flush-cut the end of the wire. With round-nose or bail-making pliers, make a loop on the wire end. This is an outside loop.

2. Grab the wire next to the loop made in Step 1 to make the second outside loop, which needs to be the same size as the loop made in Step 1. As you make the loop, guide the wire so that it loops around the pliers to the left of the loop made in Step 1, rolling the wire around until a complete loop is formed *(figure 22)*.

3. Using larger diameter bail-making pliers than you used in Steps 1 and 2, or a larger diameter on your round-nose pliers, grab the wire next to the loop made in Step 2 to make the middle loop. As you make the loop, guide the wire so that it loops around the pliers to the left of the loop made in Step 2, rolling the wire around until a complete loop is formed *(figure 23)*.

4. Using the same diameter bail-making pliers or same smaller diameter on your round-nose pliers as in Steps 1 and 2, grab the wire next to the last loop made. As you make the loop, guide the wire so that it loops around the pliers to the right of the loop made in Step 3 *(figure 24)*.

5. Repeat Step 4, then flush-cut the wire.

Straight Three-Loop Cloverleaf

For a Straight Three-Loop Cloverleaf, make three loops of the same size.

1. Working from a spool or coil of 18-gauge wire, flush-cut the wire end. With round-nose or bail-making pliers, make a loop on the wire end.

2. Turn the wire so the loop is facing in the opposite direction from which it was made, then grab the wire next to the last loop made. As you make the loop, guide the wire so that it loops around the pliers to the left of the last loop made, rolling the wire around until the wire tail is nearly even with the last loop base made *(figure 25)*. For each loop, roll the wire around until the wire tail is even with the last loop base made *(figure 26)*. After you make the third loop, flush-cut the wire.

3. With bail-making or round-nose pliers, hold the Straight Three-Loop Cloverleaf in the center loop where the wire is doubled, then push the two outside loops down with your fingers, aligning the loops *(figure 27)*.

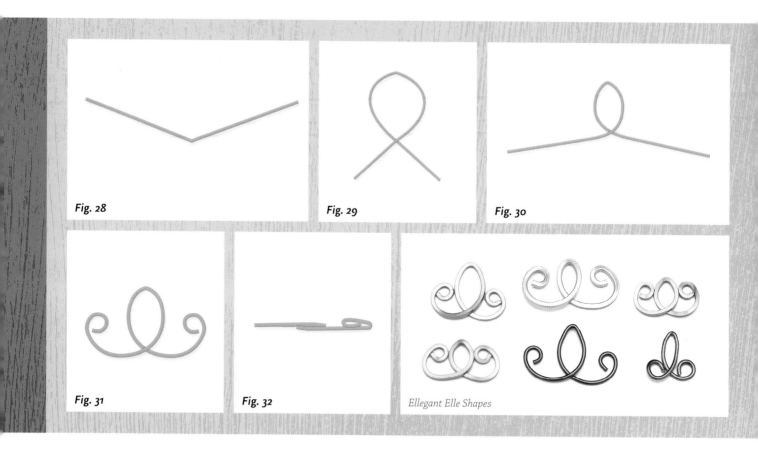

Fig. 28

Fig. 29

Fig. 30

Fig. 31

Fig. 32

Ellegant Elle Shapes

Elegant Elle

The Elegant Elle is one of my favorite shapes. It reminds me of a lowercase cursive letter L, and there are various elegant ways to fit multiples of this shape together—hence the name. For practice, straighten and flush-cut 3" (7.6 cm) of 18-gauge dead-soft wire or 3½" (8.9 cm) of 16-gauge dead-soft wire. You'll also need a permanent marker, flat-nose pliers, chain-nose pliers, a ring mandrel, and nylon-jaw wire-straightening pliers.

1. Mark the center of the wire with a permanent marker.

2. With flat-nose pliers, bend a wide V on the mark **(figure 28)**.

3. Hold the center of the V against size 1 on a ring mandrel and shape each wire end around the mandrel, crossing the wires **(figure 29)**.

   Note: *When you make several Elegant Elle shapes, it's important to cross the wires in the same way, that is, left wire end over right wire end or vice versa.*

4. With chain-nose pliers, hold the wire on one side of the bend made in Step 2. With your fingers, push the wire next to the pliers to make the loop smaller. Hold the wire on the second side of the bend and push the wire to make the loop even smaller and to keep the wire lengths equal. This makes the center of the Elegant Elle shape slightly pointed **(figure 30)**.

5. Make Arched Loops (see page 16) on each wire end **(figure 31)**.

6. Hold the center loop with nylon-jaw wire-straightening pliers and flatten the outside loops with your fingers so the shape lines up horizontally **(figure 32)**.

Fig. 33

Fig. 34

Scroll Shapes

Heart Shapes

Fig. 35

Fig. 36

Heart

I love the Heart shape. It can be turned in different directions and combined with other Heart shapes to create a variety of designs. For practice, straighten and flush-cut 4" (10.2 cm) of 18-gauge dead-soft wire. Gather a permanent marker, flat-nose pliers, and bail-making or round-nose pliers.

1. Mark the center of the wire with a permanent marker.

2. With flat-nose pliers, bend a V on the mark *(figure 33)*.

3. With bail-making or round-nose pliers, form an Arched Loop (see page 16) on each wire end, with the loops facing in toward the V *(figure 34)*. If necessary, squeeze the V together until the two Arched Loops touch.

Scroll

The Scroll is another versatile shape. The ends of the Scroll shape can be looped or arch-looped and the "body" of the Scroll can be short or long. For practice, straighten and flush-cut 2" (5.1 cm) of 18-gauge dead-soft wire.

1. Using bail-making pliers or round-nose pliers, make a loop on one wire end.

2. Make a loop on the second wire end in the opposite direction of the first loop made *(figure 35)*.

When you make a long body, the wire will remain straight. To put a slight curve in the body, as in Betty's Pendant (page 40), roll each looped end just a little bit more *(figure 36)*. (This is a great technique to use when you're fitting Scrolls into a project. If a scroll is a little too long, roll it a bit more to shorten it.)

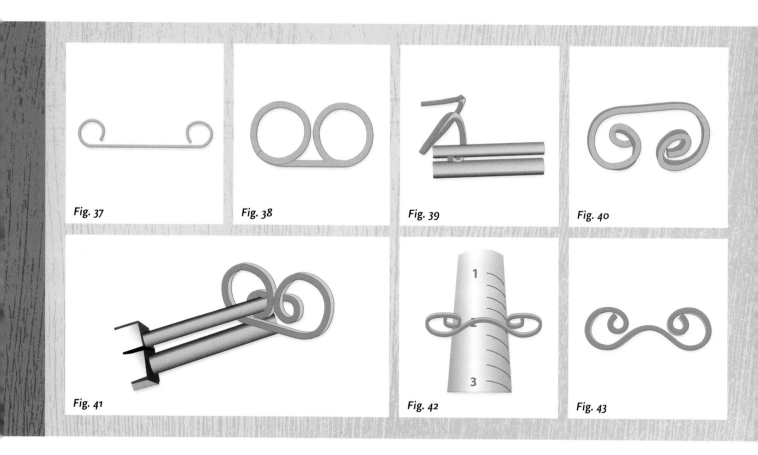

Fig. 37

Fig. 38

Fig. 39

Fig. 40

Fig. 41

Fig. 42

Fig. 43

Regal Scroll

I designed the Regal Scroll using 18-gauge wire with 7 mm and 2 mm loops. For practice, straighten and flush-cut one 2¾" (7 cm) piece of 18-gauge dead-soft wire. You'll need bail-making pliers or round-nose pliers and a ring mandrel.

1. With 7mm bail-making pliers or round-nose pliers, loop each end of one piece of wire, with the loops facing the center on the same side of the wire **(figure 37)**.

2. Continue rolling each loop, overlapping the wire base, until the loops touch in the center. Over-roll the loops equally **(figure 38)**. The wire should over-roll to the outside of the wire base, as shown, with the left loop in the front of the wire base and the right loop in the back of the wire base.

3. Open one loop by pulling it out parallel to the wire base. With 2mm bail-making pliers or round-nose pliers, make a loop on the wire end. Repeat this on the second 7 mm loop **(figures 39 and 40)**.

4. Close the 7 mm loops so they're lined up with the wire base. Your loops should be touching or nearly touching the wire base. If they're not in close proximity, grab the small loop with bail-making pliers or round-nose pliers and gently pull the loop down or roll the 7 mm loop slightly until it touches, rolling it in and down **(figure 41)**.

5. Place a ring mandrel flat on a tabletop with a towel under it so it doesn't roll. Hold the wire base against size 2 on the mandrel and press down on both loops to curve the center of the wire **(figures 42 and 43)**.

Lisa's Ring, page 66

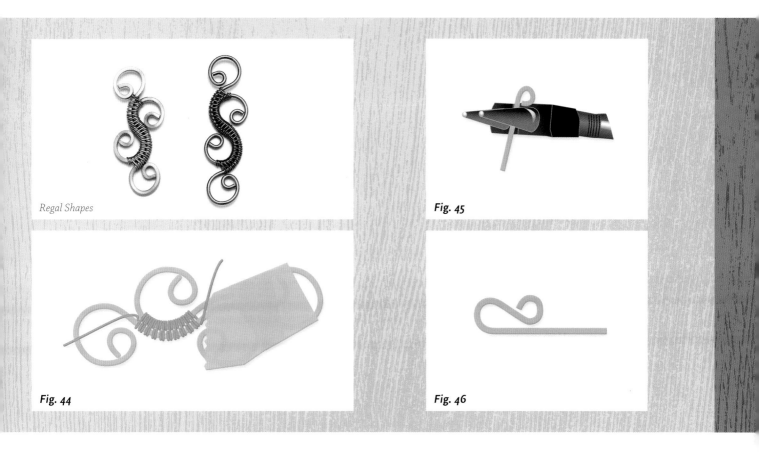

Regal Shapes

Fig. 45

Fig. 44

Fig. 46

Taping Shapes Together

It can be tricky to work with several shapes at one time, so I tape shapes together with low-stick tape (blue painter's tape). As I coil or weave, I remove and reposition the tape as needed until the project is completely coiled or woven together. Sometimes, it's easiest to arrange the shapes on a clean, hard flat surface, then press the tape over the shapes that need to be held together, leaving ample space where needed for coiling or weaving. If the ends of the tape stick to the surface, slowly peel the tape off, then wrap the ends of the tape around the shapes to the back.

Sometimes, instead of taping them, it's easier to hold the pieces in your fingers. I find this works best after I've started a project, and I'm adding one piece at a time while working multiple wire tails, as in Victoria's Pendant (page 104).

Regal Shape

The Regal Shape is made with two Regal Scrolls (page 24) woven together. To obtain shapes that are identical, it's best to make the individual Regal Scrolls first—to compare them to each other—then weave the pieces together.

Tape one end of the two Regal Scrolls together, then follow the Weave Pattern (see page 29) using 18" (45.8 cm) of 26-gauge round dead-soft wire. Weave from one outside loop to the second outside loop, removing the tape to finish weaving. Cut both wire tails *(figure 44)*.

Shepherd's Hook

I love the Shepherd's Hook shape. It's a classy way to finish the ends of wire. This shape is a featured design element in Judy's Earrings (page 88). For practice, straighten and flush-cut 4" (10.2 cm) of 18-gauge dead-soft wire.

1. With bail-making or round-nose pliers, make a small loop on one end of the wire.

2. With bail-making or round-nose pliers, grasp the wire close to the box of the pliers just under the small loop, with the loop facing toward you *(figure 45)*.

3. Roll the pliers away from you until the small loop is touching the wire, creating a hook *(figure 46)*.

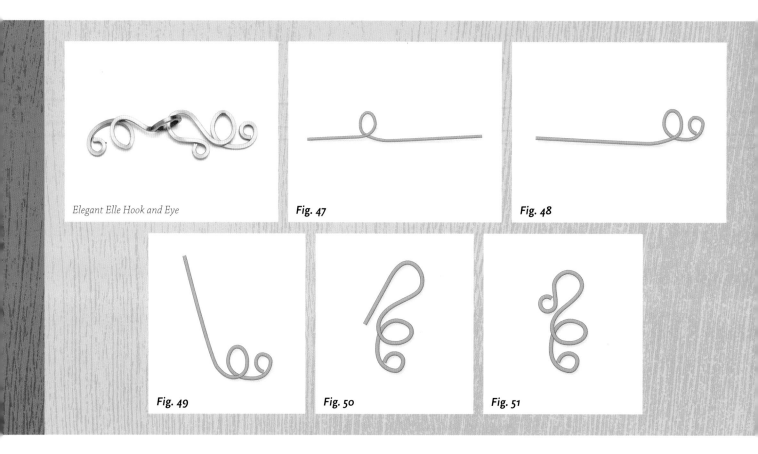

Elegant Elle Hook and Eye

Fig. 47

Fig. 48

Fig. 49

Fig. 50

Fig. 51

Elegant Elle Hook and Eye

An Elegant Elle Hook and an Elegant Elle Eye make an elegant-looking closure for a necklace or bracelet. Why purchase premade closures, when it's so easy to make one yourself? I like to use 18- or 16-gauge dead-soft wire for hooks and eyes; you can make them in various sizes by changing the length of the wire and size of the loop.

Elegant Elle Hook

1. Straighten and flush-cut 3" (7.6 cm) of 18-gauge wire, then mark the wire with a permanent marker at 1⅛" (2.9 cm) from one end. When using 16-gauge wire, flush-cut 3⅛" (7.9 cm) of wire and mark the wire at 1¼" (3.2 cm).

   Note: *These measurements are the smallest I would recommend for these wire gauges; however, longer pieces of wire can be used.*

2. With flat-nose pliers, make a bend on the mark, forming a wide V. Hold the wire on the bend against a 7mm mandrel, then shape the wire ends around the mandrel, crossing the wire ends and forming an oval-shaped loop. With chain-nose pliers, hold the wire on one side of the bend, then with your fingers, push the wire next to the pliers to make the loop smaller, pushing the wire tail until it's at a 90-degree angle to the loop. Hold the wire on the second side of the bend and push the wire to make the loop even smaller, again pushing the wire tail until it's at a 90-degree angle to the loop (*figure 47*).

3. With 2mm bail-making pliers or the small end of round-nose pliers, make a loop on the shorter wire end (*figure 48*).

4. With your fingers, hold the loop made in Step 2 and slowly push the long wire tail up, as shown (*figure 49*).

5. With 5mm bail-making pliers or the large end of round-nose pliers, grab the wire about half way in between the wire's end and the loop and roll the pliers back toward the loop made in Step 2 (*figure 50*).

6. With 2mm bail-making pliers or the small end of round-nose pliers, make a loop on the wire end, rolling the loop onto the top of the hook made in Step 4 (*figure 51*).

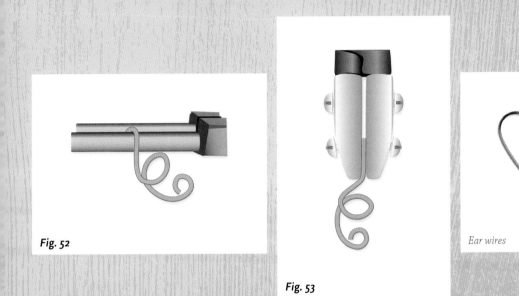

Fig. 52

Fig. 53

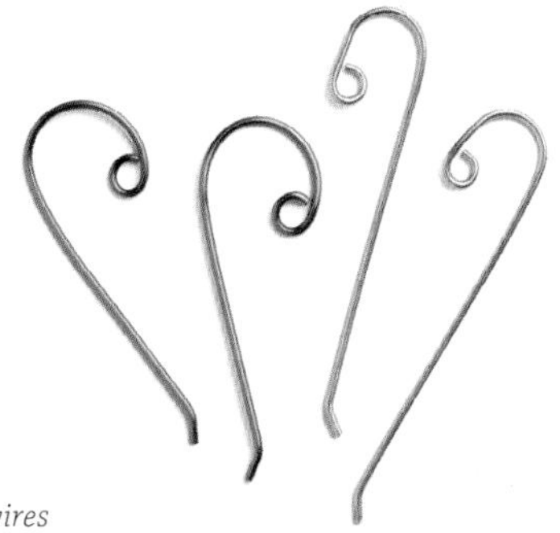

Ear wires

Elegant Elle Eye

1. Flush-cut 2⅝" (6.7 cm) of 18-gauge dead-soft wire, then mark the wire with a permanent marker 1⅛" (2.9 cm) from one end. When using 16-gauge wire, flush-cut 2¾" (7 cm) of wire and mark the wire at 1¼" (3.2 cm).

2. Follow Steps 2–4 of the Elegant Elle Hook (page 26).

3. With 5mm bail-making pliers or the large end of round-nose pliers, make a loop on the wire end, with the loop oriented to the back of the eye *(figure 52)*.

4. With chain-nose pliers or nylon-jaw wire-straightening pliers (to avoid marring the wire), grab the loop and bend it so it's centered above the loop made in Step 2 *(figure 53)*.

Ear Wires

I go in spurts with earrings—sometimes I make loads of pairs and other times, it's all about making bracelets, rings, or necklaces—so I just make ear wires when I need them. I like my wires long, but you can customize yours! I do not oxidize ear wires. Ear wires are the one finding that call for half-hard wire.

1. Straighten and flush-cut 2¼" (5.7 cm) of 20-gauge half-hard wire. Make an Arched Loop on one end of the wire (see page 16).

2. Use chain-nose pliers to make a small bend upward on the end of the wire tail.

ADDING A BEAD

In many projects in this book, a bead is added between two shapes, as in Betty's Pendant (page 40), or in a space within one shape where the frame comes together, as in the top loops of Marie's Earrings (page 48) and Victoria's Pendant (page 104). To practice adding a bead, make a Heart (page 23) or refer to Victoria's Pendant, Steps 1–3, to make the outside frame. This technique varies in some projects, as detailed in the project instructions. The bead to use is likewise detailed there.

1. With 12" (30.5 cm) of 26-gauge round dead-soft wire, leave a 1" (2.5 cm) wire tail to hold on to and coil the two loops together four or five times. Then, continue coiling two or three times around the base of one of the loops *(figure 54)*. String a 3mm bead onto the wire.

   Note: The number of times that loops or shapes are coiled together in Step 1 will vary, as will the size of loops and shapes. Coil the two loops together until there is enough space to coil in between the two loop bases or individual frame wires, as in Victoria's Pendant. Similarly, the number of times to coil around a loop base or individual base wire will vary—coil enough times to make room for the bead to hang.

2. Coil the 26-gauge wire onto the base of the second loop two or three times, coiling up toward the center coil *(figure 55)*. Cut the wire tails.

COILING

In this book, we use short pieces of wire, typically 12" (30.5 cm) at a time, to coil wire shapes together. Always leave at least a 1" (2.5 cm) tail to hold on to when you start a coil. For some projects, longer tails are required because they're used in later steps (this is indicated in individual project instructions). When you coil multiple shapes together, the idea is to try to coil as many shapes as possible together with one piece of wire, thereby minimizing wire ends on the back of the filigree designs.

As you pull the coiling wire through a small space, it can twist into a loop, which will lead to a kink. The wire can also bend and then won't pull through the opening smoothly, or worse, it will break at the bend. This is true also when you weave. Here are a few easy steps you can take to avoid this problem:
- Pull the wire slowly.
- If the wire does twist or bend, straighten it with your fingers.
- While you pull the wire end, hold the coiling/weaving wire next to the wire shape to prevent twisting or bending.

If a kink develops, uncurl and straighten coiling wire as soon as a loop begins to form; at this point, fingers should be adequate to uncurl the wire.

If you don't realize a loop has formed and the kink becomes small, you may need to use chain-nose pliers to open up and unbend the kink. However, be careful not to cut the wire!

Fig. 54

Fig. 55

If the wire is still too kinked, use nylon-jaw wire-straightening pliers to straighten the wire as best you can.

When a kink is straightened out, the wire will be weaker at that spot, and chances are good that the wire will break, especially when using fine-gauge wire, such as 26-gauge. If the wire breaks during coiling, either remove the coiled wire and begin again or simply add a new piece of wire and continue coiling.

Always try to cut the coiling wire so that it can be pressed into a space between shape wires. When you can't avoid a cut, press the cut wire end against the wire shape.

I've found that a coil can sometimes loosen as I handle a project during construction or when I shape bracelets, so it's a good idea to tighten wire tails before you cut them. I use my chain-nose pliers to pull the wire ends tightly, then cut the tails. I then open my chain-nose pliers and carefully, with the tip of the pliers, press the wire end down. Be careful with the pliers technique because the tool can slip. (I sometimes use my fingernail to press the wire end down.)

When a project is completely done, be sure to check all cut ends because the coiled cut ends can shift or lift up a bit. If this happens, press the ends down as above. If you can still feel a sharp edge, use a small flat pointed metal file to file the ends smooth (see "Filing Wire Ends," on page 30). I rarely need to file, but it's an option to keep in mind.

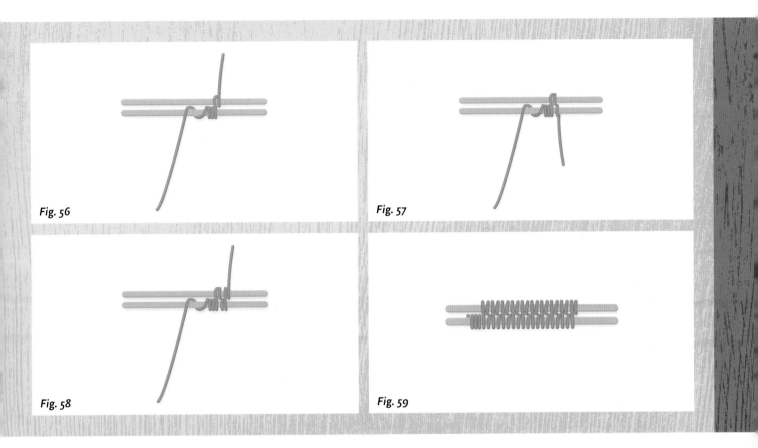

Fig. 56

Fig. 57

Fig. 58

Fig. 59

WIRE WEAVING

When you're weaving, it's always best to pull the weaving wire at a 90-degree angle to the shape wire. If the weaving wire is pulled parallel to the shape wire, there's a good chance you'll misalign one or both of the shape wires. To realign shape wires, use nylon-jaw wire-straightening pliers to gently squeeze them back into place. Avoid using chain- or flat-nose pliers because they can separate the coiling or weaving or leave tool marks. Here are some more tips:

- Always pull the weaving wire snugly around the shape wire to help prevent the wire from bulging or buckling.

- Maintain the wire's tension while you weave. Even tension will create a straight, even weave, which results in beautifully crafted jewelry. All wire has a spring to it, so it's important to push the weave together with your fingers frequently. The wire will still spring back, but the more you push the weave together, the less the wire will move.

- As with coiling, when you pull the weaving wire through a small space, it can twist into a loop and/or bend, leading to a kink. See Coiling for helpful hints to avoid or fix wire problems before kinks form.

- If the wire breaks, add more wire by coiling at least one full time around the wire frame, then proceed with weaving. After a few repetitions of the weave pattern have been made, cut the wire tail of the broken piece of wire and the new beginning wire tail.

Weave Pattern

For practice, straighten and cut two 3" (7.6 cm) pieces of 18-gauge dead-soft wire (frame wire) and 12" (30.5 cm) of 26-gauge dead-soft wire (weaving wire).

1. Leaving 1" (2.5 cm) of weaving wire to hold on to (or whatever a specific project requires), coil the weaving wire three or four times around one frame wire.

2. Hold the second frame wire next to the first frame wire, then coil one time around the second frame wire (*figure 56*).

3. Pull the weaving wire around the back of the two frame wires, then coil it one time around the first frame wire (*figure 57*).

4. Next, coil around the second frame wire once (*figure 58*).

5. Repeat Steps 3 and 4 until you reach the desired weave length. Cut the weaving wire tails (*figure 59*). With chain-nose pliers or your fingernail, press the cut wire end against the frame wire.

OXIDIZING WIRE

Silver Black and liver of sulfur (LOS) are chemical solutions that oxidize metals for an antiqued appearance. I prefer Silver Black over LOS because its odor is milder. Either product should be used in a well-ventilated room and/or with a breathing mask on. Do not immerse porous beads in either of these chemicals because they will absorb the liquid and may be discolored.

To oxidize wire, you'll need a round bottle for coiling 26-gauge wire, Silver Black or LOS, a bowl, tongs or tweezers, a towel, and 0000 steel wool.

1. Coil the length of wire required for the project. I like to oxidize my wire before making my jewelry. I cut the total required length of wire of all gauges for a particular project, wind it into a coil, and then oxidize the wire. I do this because my coiled filigree techniques involve many small pieces of wire; it's much easier and less time-consuming to oxidize and polish a long piece of wire than to treat many small shapes. I also find that silver wire looks more consistent when it's oxidized first.

2. Set your container inside a sink with the drain closed and a small amount of water in the sink. I use a 6½" (16.5 cm) square flat-bottomed plastic container to oxidize the wire. Be sure the larger-gauge wire coils fit easily inside the container. Don't wedge wire into a too-small container—when you pour the chemical in, you don't want a wire end to pop up out of the container and possibly splatter the solution.

3. Place the coiled wire in a container, then pour the chemical into the container. How much to pour? I use a large bowl, so I pour in enough of the chemical solution to cover about half the wire, then use tongs to turn the wire over or move it around within the container until it's evenly oxidized.

4. Remove the wire with tongs, remove the container from the sink, and place the wire in the sink water. Rinse well.

5. Place the wire on a towel and pat dry or allow to air dry.

6. Follow the manufacturer's recommendations for disposing of the chemicals. Wash tongs and container with dish soap.

7. Use steel wool to polish the wire. Polishing removes oxidization but be aware of how much chemical you're removing and how dark or light you want your wire to be. I've found that it's very easy to over-polish 26-gauge wire if I squeeze the steel wool to grasp the wire and remove too much oxidation. If you find this to be a problem, you can weave or coil 26-gauge wire first, then polish or leave it darker than the larger-gauge wires as a contrast—or just practice a few times to avoid over-polishing. After a project is complete, you may need to polish it a bit more to lighten any overly dark areas.

Filing Wire Ends

If you can still feel a sharp edge after you cut the wire tails, hold a flat pointed metal file against the cut edge, angled slightly downward if possible, and file in the direction of the wire end, not against the wire end. Lift the file, place it back at the starting point, and file in the same direction, repeating this until the wire end is smooth. If possible, tilt the file so that it is against the side of the wire end and file that smooth, using the same motion as before. Repeat this action on the second side of the wire end.

Caution!

When oxidizing, I always place the container in a sink, but Silver Black or LOS may oxidize a metal sink or drain. I have a porcelain sink with a metal drain. I once oxidized some silver and had a very small amount of chemical left, so I dumped it down the drain. Now, about a quarter of my metal drain is oxidized—another learning experience, or, as my daughter Jules would say, "It's just another blonde moment in a lifetime of many." Always follow the manufacturer's recommendations for disposing of these chemical solutions.

Oxidizing Thin Wire

To oxidize 26-gauge wire, coil the wire around the base of a small bottle such as a vitamin bottle. To remove the coiled wire, hold the wire ends against the bottle and slide the coil off, then wrap both wire ends around the coil to secure the wire *(figure 60)*; Otherwise, your coil will pop open and you'll end up with wire all over the place. For all other gauges, I shape the wire into large loops by hand, creating a coil, but I don't wrap the ends around the coil.

Fig. 60

Franchezka's Necklace, page 128

The Projects

Janice's Pendant

The inspiration for this pendant was the gorgeous golden rutilated quartz briolette I found at a bead show. The flowing lines of the Elegant Elle shapes spotlight the stone without overpowering it. I designed the pendant in honor of my mom, Janice, who always wore my jewelry with pride.

Techniques

◊ *Elegant Elle (page 22)*
◊ *Arched Loop (page 16)*
◊ *Coiling (page 28)*
◊ *Adding a Bead (page 28)*
◊ *Wrapped Loop (page 16)*
◊ *Elegant Elle Hook (page 26)*
◊ *Elegant Elle Eye (page 27)*
◊ *Jump Rings (optional; page 18)*

Finished Measurements

Pendant with dangles: 1⅞" (4.8 cm); **chain with clasp:** 20" (50.8 cm)

Project Notes

I used 18-gauge square sterling silver dead-soft wire for the Elegant Elle (EE) shapes and the bottom U shape. I used 26-gauge round sterling silver dead-soft wire for coiling. My briolette is golden rutilated quartz, which I purchased from Bead Palace, and the Swarovski bicone beads are light topaz and crystal. My pendant loops are 2 mm.

PENDANT MATERIALS

• 9" (22.9 cm) of 18-gauge square dead-soft wire
• 18" (45.8 cm) of 26-gauge round dead-soft wire
• 1 glass, crystal, or stone 13.6 × 22mm flat top-drilled briolette
• 7 crystal 4mm bicone beads
• 7 sterling silver 2" (5.1 cm) head pins
• ¼" (6.4 mm) of commercial chain

CHAIN AND HOOK MATERIALS

• 34" (86.4 cm) of commercial chain
• 5⅝" (14.3 cm) of 18-gauge square dead-soft wire
• 12" (30.5 cm) of 24-gauge round dead-soft wire
• 2 crystal 4mm bicone beads
• 1 crystal 6mm bicone bead
• 2 crystal 5mm flat bicone beads
• 12 round 4mm 20-gauge jump rings, store-bought or handmade
• 2 round 6mm 16-gauge jump rings, store-bought or handmade

TOOLS

• Nylon-jaw wire-straightening pliers
• Flush cutters
• Ring mandrel
• 2/2.5, 3/5 and 7/9mm bail-making pliers or round-nose pliers
• Flat-nose pliers
• Chain-nose pliers
• Ruler
• Low-stick tape
• Permanent marker

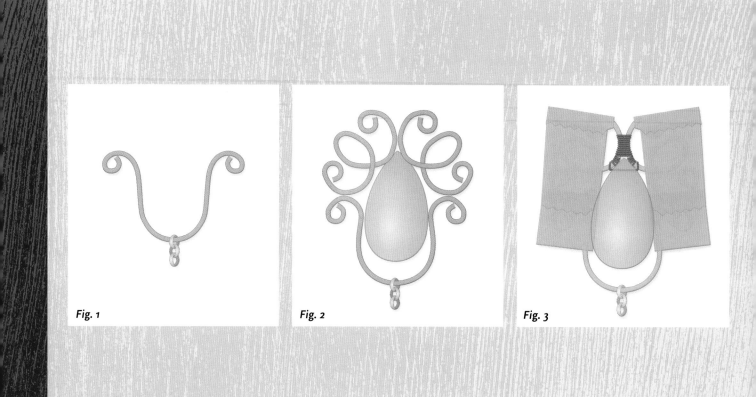

Fig. 1   Fig. 2   Fig. 3

1. Make two EE shapes using 3" (7.6 cm) of 18-gauge square dead-soft wire. Set aside.

2. To make the bottom U shape of the pendant, straighten and flush-cut 3" (7.6 cm) of 18-gauge dead-soft wire. Mark the center of the wire with a permanent marker.

3. Hold the mark against size 1 on a ring mandrel and push the wire ends around to form a U.

   Note: At its widest point, my briolette is 13.6 mm. If your briolette is wider, shape the U on size 1, then expand the U curve by holding it on a slightly larger ring mandrel size and pushing the wire ends toward each other to form the U. Repeat this until the shape fits around the bottom of your briolette. If your briolette is smaller than 13.6 mm, measure the width and use a mandrel that is at least 2 mm larger than the briolette, such as a permanent marker.

4. With 2mm bail-making or round-nose pliers, make an Arched Loop on one wire end. Slide ¼" (6.4 mm) of chain onto the second wire end, then make a 2mm Arched Loop on the second wire end, with both loops going toward the outside of the U *(figure 1)*.

5. Lay the shapes and briolette on a hard, flat, clean surface. The top of the briolette determines the angle of the EE shapes *(figure 2)*.

   Note: The Arched Loops of the U shape will be adjusted in Step 8, if necessary, after the briolette is attached.

6. Tape the sides of the shapes together. Remove the briolette, then tape across the shapes for stability. Leave the top center of the EE shapes exposed for coiling.

7. With 9" (22.9 cm) of 26-gauge round dead-soft wire, coil the EE shapes together ten to twelve times or until there is enough room to coil an individual curve of the Arched Loops. Remove the tape as necessary and add the briolette *(figure 3)*.

8. Remove all the tape. If there is space between the bottom of your briolette and the U shape, roll each Arched Loop equally until there's just enough space for the chain to move freely.

9. Tape one side of the U shape and with 9" (22.9 cm) of 26-gauge round dead-soft wire, coil the curve of one EE shape to the curve of the U shape five to six times *(figure 4)*. Cut the wire tails.

10. Remove the tape and coil the curves of the second EE shape and the U shape five to six times. Cut the wire tails.

Fig. 4

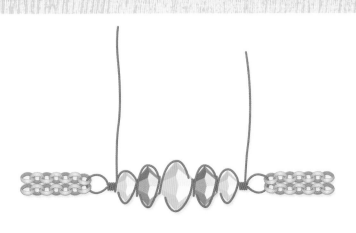

Fig. 5

11. Slide a 4mm bicone bead onto a head pin. Make a Wrapped Loop, but before wrapping the loop closed, attach the loop to a link on the ¼" (6.4 mm) chain. Repeat this step six times to create the cluster dangle at the bottom of the pendant.

12. Make an Elegant Elle Hook with 3" (7.6 cm) of 18-gauge square dead-soft wire and an Elegant Elle Eye with 2⅝" (6.7 cm) of 18-gauge square dead-soft wire. Set aside.

13. Cut two 2" (5.1 cm) pieces of chain. Cut 12" (30.5 cm) of 24-gauge round dead-soft wire. Mark the wire at 5" (12.7 cm) with a permanent marker, then make a 90-degree bend with flat-nose pliers on the mark. Make a Wrapped Loop, but before wrapping the loop closed, attach the loop to one end of each chain, then wrap the loop closed. Do not cut the wire tail.

14. Cut two 6" (15.2 cm) pieces of chain and set aside. Slide a 4mm bicone bead, 5mm flat bicone bead, 6mm bicone bead, 5mm flat bicone bead, and 4mm bicone bead onto the 24-gauge round dead-soft wire. Make a Wrapped Loop, but before wrapping the loop closed, attach the loop to one end of each 6" (15.2 cm) chain, then wrap the loop closed. Do not cut the wire tail.

15. Wrap one wire tail around each bicone bead. Next, wrap the second wire tail around each bicone bead, then wrap that tail around the Wrapped Loop, creating a double wrap **(figure 5)**.

16. Wrap the second wire tail from Step 15 around the Wrapped Loop. Cut both wire tails.

17. Attach two 4mm jump rings to a top EE loop. Attach two 4mm jump rings to these jump rings and through both chain ends of the 2" (5.1 cm) piece of chain. This is one-half of the chain for the necklace.
   Note: *If you're using a flat chain, such as flat cable, only one set of 4mm jump rings is required.*

18. Cut two 9" (22.9 cm) pieces of chain or the length that matches the opposite side of the necklace. Repeat Step 17, attaching the second set of 4mm jump rings to one end of each 9" (22.9 cm) piece of chain.

19. Attach two 4mm jump rings through the chain ends on one side of the necklace. Attach one 6mm jump ring to these 4mm jump rings and through the base loop of the Elegant Elle Hook. Repeat to attach the base loop of the Elegant Elle Eye to the other half of the necklace.
   Note: *If you're using a flat chain, such as flat cable, only the 6mm jump rings are required for each chain end.*

Abby's Bracelet

I created this design for fellow wire artisan Abby Hook as a thank-you for being such a wonderful friend and for always being so encouraging. You can easily lengthen or shorten the bracelet to customize it for a special friend.

Techniques

◊ *Elegant Elle Hook (page 26)*
◊ *Elegant Elle Eye (page 27)*
◊ *Regal Loop (page 17)*
◊ *Coiling (page 28)*
◊ *Jump Rings (optional; page 18)*

Finished Measurement

7" (17.8 cm)

Project Notes

I used 21-gauge square antique copper ParaWire for the filigree pieces and 18-gauge square wire for the Elegant Elle Hook and Elegant Elle Eye. To make your bracelet longer, add filigree pieces or use a chain extender. To make it shorter, subtract filigree pieces or omit the Elegant Elle Eye. The length of wire and number of jump rings and beads you need is determined by how many filigree pieces you make.

MATERIALS

- 6" (15.2 cm) of 18-gauge square dead-soft wire
- 30"–36" (76.2–91.4 cm) of 21-gauge square dead-soft wire
- 5'–6' (1.5–1.8 m) of 26-gauge round dead-soft wire
- 5 or 6 melon-shaped or round 10mm beads
- 10–12 round 4mm beads
- 20–24 round 4mm 20-gauge jump rings, store-bought or handmade
- Two 7mm 16-gauge jump rings (optional)

TOOLS

- Nylon-jaw wire-straightening pliers
- Flush cutters
- Flat-nose pliers
- Chain-nose pliers
- 2/2.5, 3/5, and 7/9mm bail-making pliers or round-nose pliers
- Ruler
- Low-stick tape
- Permanent marker
- Gridded composition paper

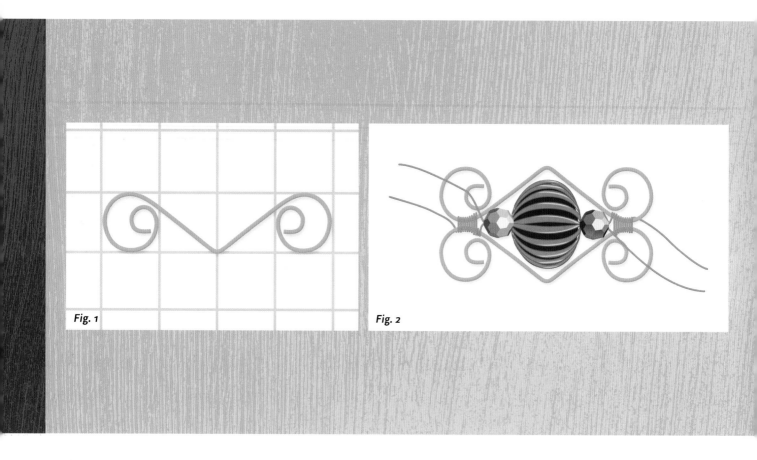

Fig. 1

Fig. 2

1. Make an Elegant Elle Hook with 3" (7.6 cm) of 18-gauge square dead-soft wire and an Elegant Elle Eye using 2⅝" (6.7 cm) of 18-gauge square dead-soft wire.

2. Straighten and flush-cut two 3" (7.6 cm) pieces of 21-gauge square dead-soft wire. Mark the center of each piece with a permanent marker.

3. Take one 3" (7.6 cm) piece of wire and make Regal Loops with 5mm and 2mm bail-making pliers or round-nose pliers on each wire end with the loops on the same side of the wire. Repeat this step on the second 3" (7.6 cm) piece of wire.

4. With flat-nose pliers, make a bend on the permanent marker mark, forming a wide V, with the Regal Loops on the outside of the V *(figure 1)*. The tip of the V and the Regal Loops should line up. Place the wire on gridded composition paper to check the alignment. Repeat this step for the second piece of wire.

5. With low-stick tape, tape the two pieces together on one end, with the V of each piece facing out. Leave the Regal Loops on the other end exposed for coiling.

6. With 12" (30.5 cm) of 26-gauge round dead-soft wire, coil the two Regal Loops on one end together five or six times, then coil one Regal Loop wire one time. Do not cut the wire tails.

7. Remove the tape. Repeat Step 6 on the second two Regal Loops. String a 4mm bead, a 10mm bead, and a 4mm bead onto one wire tail, then thread the tail wire on the opposite end through the beads in the opposite direction, so the wires cross inside the bead. Pull the wire tails until the beads are between the two V-shaped wires *(figure 2)*.

8. Coil one wire tail one time around the opposing Regal Loop wire, toward the coil made in Step 6. Repeat this with the second wire tail. Coil the second wire tail one more time. Coil the first wire tail a second time.
   Note: Working back and forth ensures that you don't pull the wire too tightly and displace the beads. Cut the four wire tails.

9. To shape the beaded filigree piece, hold each end in between your fingers and gently bend the ends downward equally until, when placed on a flat surface, the Regal Loops touch the flat surface *(figure 3)*.

10. Repeat Steps 2–9 one time. Use the remaining 26-gauge round dead-soft wire from Steps 6 and 8 or cut additional 12" (30.5 cm) pieces as needed.

11. Attach one end of the two beaded filigree pieces with four 4mm jump rings, attaching a Regal Loop to a Regal Loop with two jump rings and using the remaining two jump rings to attach the second set of Regal Loops.

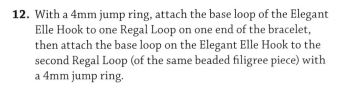

Fig. 3

12. With a 4mm jump ring, attach the base loop of the Elegant Elle Hook to one Regal Loop on one end of the bracelet, then attach the base loop on the Elegant Elle Hook to the second Regal Loop (of the same beaded filigree piece) with a 4mm jump ring.

13. Repeat Steps 2–11 until you achieve the desired length for the bracelet.

14. With a 4mm jump ring, attach the base loop of the Elegant Elle Eye to one Regal Loop on the opposite end of the bracelet, then attach the base loop of the Elegant Elle Eye to the second Regal Loop with a 4mm jump ring. If you didn't make an Elegant Elle Eye for the Elegant Elle Hook, then attach jump rings for the hook to hook through: Attach one 7mm 16-gauge jump ring to a Regal Loop and one 7mm jump ring to the second Regal Loop.

Betty's Pendant

An emerald briolette framed by flowing silver Scrolls is a magnificent focal point my Aunt Betty would have loved. This three-point pendant can be easily transformed into an equally stunning pair of earrings (see page 43).

Techniques

◊ *Oxidizing Wire (page 30)*

◊ *Scroll (page 23)*

◊ *Coiling (page 28)*

◊ *Adding a Bead (page 28)*

◊ *Elegant Elle Hook (page 26)*

◊ *Jump Rings (optional; page 18)*

Finished Measurements

Pendant: 1½" (3.8 cm); **chain and clasp:** 23" (58.4 cm)

Project Notes

For the pendant, I made all the loops the same size (3 mm). If you want to make different size loops for the pendant Scrolls (S-shapes), be sure to make the same size loops on the pieces that are duplicates. It's best to oxidize the wire, jump rings, and chain components before you make the piece.

PENDANT MATERIALS

- 9¼" (23.5 cm) of 16-gauge square dead-soft wire
- 3'–4' (91.4–1.2 m) of 26-gauge round dead-soft wire
- 1 glass, crystal, or stone 10mm top-drilled briolette

CHAIN AND HOOK MATERIALS

- 4' (1.2 m) of 16-gauge square dead-soft wire
- 72 round 18-gauge 5mm jump rings, store-bought or handmade
- 2 round 18-gauge 7mm jump rings or size needed for your hook to fit through
- 4" (10.2 cm) of 18-gauge square dead-soft wire or the gauge wire that will fit through the rondelle holes
- 2 faceted 6mm rondelles
- 2 round 6mm washers

TOOLS

- Nylon-jaw wire-straightening pliers
- Flush cutters
- 2/2.5, 3/5, and 7/9mm bail-making pliers or round-nose pliers
- Ruler
- Low-stick tape
- Silver Black or LOS, bowl, and tongs
- 0000 steel wool

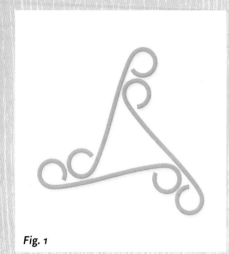

Fig. 1

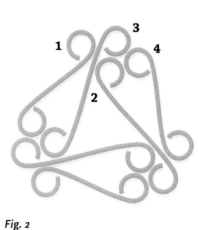

Fig. 2

Fig. 3

1. Straighten and flush-cut three 2" (5.1 cm) pieces and three 1¾" (4.4 cm) pieces of 16-gauge square dead-soft wire. Using 3mm bail-making pliers or round-nose pliers, make a loop on each end of one wire going in opposite directions, forming a Scroll shape. Over-roll the loops slightly to form an S-shaped curve in each Scroll. Repeat with the remaining five pieces of wire.

2. Lay the 2" (5.1 cm) pieces on a clean hard flat surface as shown in *figure 1*.

3. Lay the 1¾" (4.4 cm) pieces next to the 2" (5.1 cm) pieces as shown in *figure 2*.

   Note: In Steps 4–7, refer to this illustration for the numbering sequence of the loops that are being coiled together.

4. Tape the Scrolls together, leaving one set of loops exposed. With 12" (30.5 cm) of 26-gauge round dead-soft wire, leave a 1" (2.5 cm) tail and coil loops 1 and 2 together four to five times, ending the coil by bringing the wire tail up inside loop 2. Do not cut the wire tail *(figure 3)*.

5. With the remaining wire, coil loops 2 and 3 together four to five times, ending the coil by bringing the wire tail up inside loop 2. Do not cut the wire tail.

6. With the remaining wire, coil loops 2 and 4 together four to five times. Cut the beginning and ending wire tails.

   Note: Cut an additional 12" (30.5 cm) of 26-gauge round dead-soft wire as needed.

7. Coil loops 3 and 4 together four to five times. Cut the beginning and ending wire tails *(figure 4)*.

8. Remove and reposition the tape. Repeat Steps 4–7 one time on a second set of four loops.

9. For the final set of four loops, cut 18" (45.7 cm) of 26-gauge round dead-soft wire and leaving an 8" (20.3 cm) tail, repeat Steps 4–7 but do not cut the 8" (20.3 cm) tail.

10. With the 8" (20.3 cm) tail, add a bead, coiling loop 2 and the body of loop 3 together three to four times. Continue coiling the body of loop 3 until there is enough space for the briolette to hang, finishing by coiling up the body of loop 2 *(figure 5)*.

11. *Scroll Chain:* Make an Elegant Elle Hook with 3⅛" (7.9 cm) of 16-gauge square dead-soft wire. Make 34 Scrolls with 1¼" (3.2 cm) of 16-gauge square dead-soft wire and 2.5 mm loops.

Fig. 4

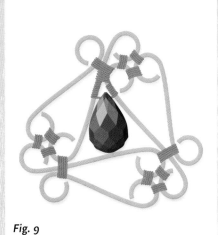

Fig. 9

Variation

To make a pair of earrings, simply attach the pendant shapes to ear wires with short lengths of chain and jump rings. Here, I switched up the design by using copper wire and amethyst briolettes, but you can certainly use the same materials as the pendant to create a matching set. I used 18-gauge square dead-soft wire. For each earring, I cut three pieces at 1½" (3.8 cm) each and three pieces at 1¼" (3.2 cm) each.

12. With 4" (10.2 cm) of 18-gauge square dead-soft wire, make a 2.5 mm simple loop on one wire end. Slide one 6mm rondelle, two washers, and the second 6mm rondelle onto the wire. Make a matching simple loop on the second wire end.

13. Attach two Scrolls together with two 5mm jump rings. Attach the Elegant Elle Hook to one Scroll with two 5mm jump rings. Attach the second Scroll to a top loop on Betty's Pendant with two 5mm jump rings. Set aside.

14. Assemble five Scrolls together with pairs of 5mm jump rings. Attach the rondelles/washers to the last Scroll in this section with two 5mm jump rings. Continue assembling the chain with pairs of 5mm jump rings until you reach your desired length, ending with two 7mm jump rings. Attach the other end of this section to a top loop on the Trinity pendant with two 5mm jump rings.

Trish's Necklace

I love the eye-catching porcelain pendants and beads from Clay River Designs! For this piece, I wanted the focus to be on the pendant and beads, not the wire, so I created a simple chain of beads and Regal Loops and left the pendant alone to shine. It's truly a quick and easy project to make. I know my friend Trish, and anyone you make it for, will love it.

Techniques
◊ *Elegant Elle Hook (page 26)*
◊ *Elegant Elle Eye (page 27)*
◊ *Regal Loop (page 17)*
◊ *Jump Rings (optional; page 18)*

Finished Measurement
17½" (44.5 cm)

Project Notes
I used 20-gauge round sterling silver dead-soft wire to make the Regal Loops.

MATERIALS
- 6" (15.2 cm) of 18-gauge round dead-soft wire
- 4' (1.2 m) of 20-gauge round dead-soft wire
- 1 ceramic 1¼" (3.2 cm) round pendant
- 18 ceramic 4mm rondelle beads
- 36 round 2mm beads
- 40 round 3mm 20-gauge jump rings, store-bought or handmade

TOOLS
- Nylon-jaw wire-straightening pliers
- Flush cutters
- Chain-nose pliers
- 2/2.5, 3/5 and 7/9mm bail-making pliers or round-nose pliers
- Permanent marker
- Ruler

Fig. 1

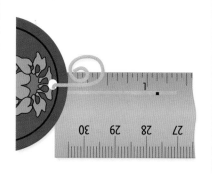

Fig. 2

Fig. 3

1. Make an Elegant Elle Hook with 3" (7.6 cm) of 18-gauge round dead-soft wire and an Elegant Elle Eye using 2⅝" (14.3 cm) of 18-gauge round dead-soft wire.

2. *Pendant Bail:* Straighten and flush-cut 3" (7.6 cm) of 20-gauge round dead-soft wire. Make a Regal Loop on one end of the wire with 5mm and 2mm bail-making or round-nose pliers.

3. Hold the wire against the pendant, with the Regal Loop resting on top of the pendant. Use the permanent marker to mark where the wire intersects the pendant hole **(figure 1)**.

4. Slide the wire through the pendant hole until the permanent marker mark is just inside the hole. While you hold the Regal Loop at the top of the pendant, grab the wire tail and bend it up. Next, measuring from the top of the pendant, mark the wire tail at 1⅛" (2.9 cm).

   Note: If you're not using 5mm and 2mm bail-making or round-nose pliers to make the Regal Loop, you'll need to calculate how much wire you need to make your loop. To do so, see the instructions for P-Shaped Loops (page 14). The length of wire needed to make the loop is at the mark where the end of the wire is on the over-rolled part of the loop (figure 2).

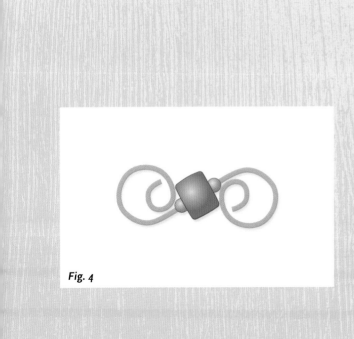

Fig. 4

5. Flush-cut the wire on the mark. Bend the wire at a 90-degree angle to the pendant, then make a Regal Loop with 5mm and 2mm bail-making or round-nose pliers. Bend the wire back to its original position with the Regal Loop on top of the pendant.

6. With nylon-jaw wire-straightening pliers, squeeze the Regal Loops together so they sit on top of the pendant **(figure 3)**.

7. *Chain:* To make the double–Regal Loop chain pieces, you'll need to do some math. Each 5/2mm Regal Loop uses 1⅛" (2.9 cm) of wire. Multiplying this by two equals 2¼" (5.7 cm). To add a 2mm, 4mm, and 2mm bead equals ¼" (6.4 mm). Adding this number to 2¼" (5.7 cm) equals 2½" (6.4 cm).

   Straighten and flush-cut 2½" (6.4 cm) of 20-gauge round dead-soft wire. Make a Regal Loop on one end of the wire with 5mm and 2mm bail-making or round-nose pliers. String a 2mm, 4mm, and 2mm bead onto the wire, then make a Regal Loop on the second end of the wire **(figure 4)**.

8. Repeat Step 7 seventeen times, for a total of eighteen double–Regal Loop chain pieces.

9. *Assembly:* Connect two double–Regal Loop chain pieces together using two 3mm jump rings. Repeat this until a total of nine chain pieces are connected. This is one half of the chain. Repeat this on the remaining nine chain pieces for the second half of the chain.

10. With two 3mm jump rings, connect one half of the chain to one Regal Loop on the bail. Repeat with the second half of the chain, connecting the chain to the second Regal Loop on the bail.

11. Use two 3mm jump rings to attach the base loop of the Elegant Elle Hook to the end of one chain. Repeat to attach the base loop of the Elegant Elle Eye to the end of the other chain.

Marie's Earrings

Small hearts nestle within larger hearts to create a romantic design. Oxidized silver accented with semiprecious onyx briolettes and black crystals are the perfect match. I named these earrings for my Aunt "Rie-Rie," a most kind and loving woman.

Techniques

◊ *Oxidizing Wire (page 30)*

◊ *Heart (page 23)*

◊ *Arched Loops (page 16)*

◊ *Jump Rings (optional; page 18)*

◊ *Coiling (page 28)*

◊ *Adding a Bead (page 28)*

◊ *Ear Wires (page 27)*

◊ ***Variation:*** *Three-Loop Cloverleaf (page 20)*

Finished Measurement

2½" (6.4 cm) including ear wire

Project Notes

I used 18-gauge square sterling silver dead-soft wire for these earrings, making 3 mm loops for the large Heart shapes and 2 mm loops for the small Heart shapes. It's best to oxidize the wire, jump rings, and chain components (except the wire used for ear wires) before you make the piece.

MATERIALS

- 13½"(34.3 cm) of 18-gauge square dead-soft wire
- 4½" (11.4 cm) of 20-gauge round half-hard wire (ear wires)
- 4'–5' (1.2–1.5 m) of 26-gauge round dead-soft wire
- 4 crystal or glass 3mm bicone beads
  Note: *Bicone-shaped beads fit into the small space really well. Semiprecious stones are too large for this design.*
- 2 crystal, glass, or semiprecious 14mm top-drilled briolettes
- 3" (7 cm) of commercial chain
- 2 round 4mm 20-gauge jump rings, store-bought or handmade

VARIATION MATERIALS

Use the same material as above with these exceptions:

- No chain
- 15" to 16" (38.1 to 40.6 cm) of 18-gauge round dead-soft wire
- 4 crystal, glass, or semiprecious 3mm beads
- 4 round 4mm 20-gauge jump rings, store-bought or handmade

TOOLS

- Silver Black or LOS, bowl, and tongs
- 0000 steel wool
- Nylon-jaw wire-straightening pliers
- Flush cutters
- 2/2.5mm and 3/5mm bail-making pliers or round-nose pliers
- Chain-nose pliers
- Ruler
- Low-stick tape
- Permanent marker

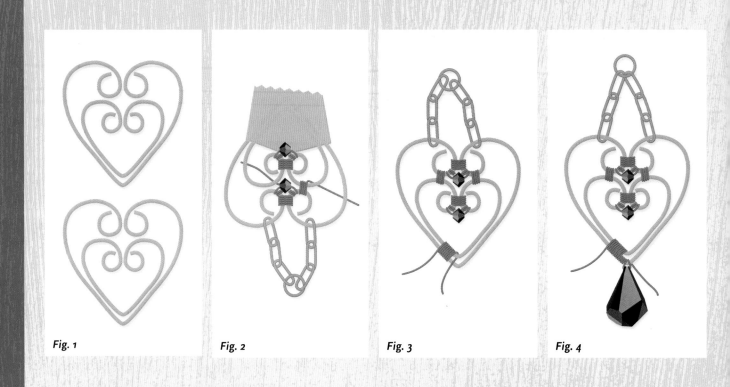

Fig. 1   Fig. 2   Fig. 3   Fig. 4

1. Make two large Heart shapes with 4" (10.2 cm) of 18-gauge square dead-soft wire and two small Heart shapes with 2¾" (7 cm) of 18-gauge square dead-soft wire.

2. Place the small Heart shapes inside the large Heart shapes and if needed, adjust the Arched Loops until the shapes fit together *(figure 1)*.

3. Cut two ¾" (1.9 cm) segments of chain. Open a loop of one of the large Heart shapes as you would open a jump ring, then slide one end of both pieces of chain onto the shape. Close the loop.

4. With 12" (30.5 cm) of 26-gauge round dead-soft wire, coil the two loops of the large Heart shape together five times, then add a 3mm bicone bead, coiling the wire three times on each side of the bead.

   Note: Cut additional 12" (30.5 cm) lengths of 26-gauge round dead-soft wire as needed.

5. Coil the loops of the two small Heart shapes together four times and add a 3mm bicone bead, coiling the wire three times on each side of the bead. Cut the wire tails.

6. Slide the chains to the top of the large Heart shape, with one chain at the top of each arch. Connect the top of the two chains together with a 4mm jump ring.

7. Place the small Heart shape inside the large Heart shape, then tape the bottom of the shapes together.

8. With 26-gauge round dead-soft wire and starting next to where the bicone bead is attached, coil one of the loops of the large Heart shape to the arch of the small Heart shape four times. Turn the Heart shapes upside down to do this, coiling left to right in order to get the coil as close to the bicone-bead coil as possible *(figure 2)*.

9. Cut the wire tails. Repeat Step 8 on the second loop and arch. Again, start the coil next to where the bicone bead is attached, coiling left to right. Cut the wire tails.

10. Remove the tape. With 12" (30.5 cm) of 26-gauge round dead-soft wire, coil the bottom of the Heart shapes together seven to eight times. Just before the bend in the small Heart-shape V, bring the wire up in between the two Heart shapes *(figure 3)*.

11. Coil the large Heart shape two to three times up to its V, then string a briolette onto the wire. Thread the wire in between the two Heart shapes, positioning the briolette so it hangs in the center of the Heart frames *(figure 4)*.

12. Coil the large Heart shape two to three times, then coil both Heart shapes together seven to eight times. Cut the beginning and ending wire tails.

13. Repeat Steps 3–12 for the second earring.

14. With 20-gauge round half-hard wire, make two ear wires. Attach an ear wire to the 4mm jump ring on each chain.

Variation

A few simple substitutions create a remarkably different look. Here, I used 18-gauge round antique copper ParaWire with ruby beads. I also turned the inner Heart shapes upside down and connected the earrings to the ear wires with a Three-Loop Cloverleaf, instead of a chain.

1. Make two large Heart shapes with 4" (10.2 cm) of 18-gauge round dead-soft wire and two small Heart shapes with 2½" (6.4 cm) of 18-gauge round dead-soft wire. When you make the loops of the small Heart shapes, leave them slightly open for ease of coiling.

2. Place the small Heart shapes upside down inside the large Heart shapes and adjust the arched loops as needed until the shapes fit together *(figure 5)*.

3. With 12" (30.5 cm) of 26-gauge round dead soft-wire and holding a small Heart shape upside down, coil the small Heart loops together five times, then add a 3mm semiprecious bead, coiling the wire five times on each side of the bead. Cut the wire tails *(figure 6)*.

4. Next, coil the loops of the large Heart shape together five times. Place the small Heart shape upside down inside the large Heart shape, then tape the bottom of the shapes together. Coil around the loop of the large Heart shape and the base of the small Heart shape four times then add a 3mm semiprecious bead, coiling five times on each side of the bead *(figure 7)*.

5. Cut the wire tails and remove the tape. With 12" (30.5 cm) of 26-gauge round dead-soft wire, coil the arch of the small Heart shape to the large Heart shape six times then continue coiling the large Heart shape to just before the V, add a briolette, then coil the second side of the large Heart shape, and finishing by coiling the two shapes together. Cut the wire tails *(figure 8)*.

6. Make a Three-Loop Cloverleaf with 18-gauge round dead soft-wire. Attach this to the top of the large Heart shape with two 4mm jump rings.

7. Repeat Steps 3–6 for the second earring.

8. With 20-gauge round half-hard wire, make two ear wires. Attach each ear wire to the center of each Cloverleaf.

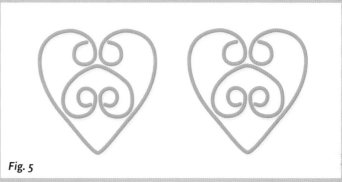

Fig. 5

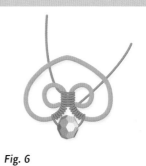

Fig. 6

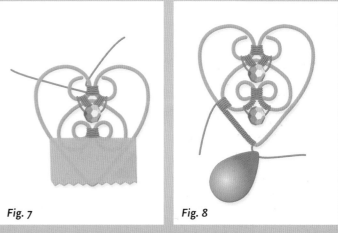

Fig. 7   *Fig. 8*

Misti's Bracelet

With swirls of Regal Shapes and beautiful blue crystals, this bracelet is fit to be worn by a princess, or by a very artsy, talented woman, my sister Misti.

Techniques

◊ *Oxidizing Wire (page 30)*
◊ *Elegant Elle Hook (page 26)*
◊ *Elegant Elle Eye (page 27)*
◊ *Regal Scroll (page 24)*
◊ *Regal Shape (page 25)*
◊ *Weave Pattern (page 29)*
◊ *Coiling (page 28)*

Finished Measurements

7¼" (18.4 cm) including hook and eye, plus 1" (2.5 cm) chain extender

Project Notes

I flush-cut 2¾" (6 cm) of dead-soft wire for each Regal Scroll and made 2 mm loops. You'll make two Regal Scrolls and weave them together for each Regal Shape. Because the looped ends of the Regal Shapes are offset, I coiled the Elegant Elle Hook and Elegant Elle Eye to the bracelet which balances the ends. It's best to oxidize the wire and chain components before you make the piece.

MATERIALS

- 40" (1 m) of 18-gauge square dead-soft wire
- 14'–15' (4.3–4.6 m) of 26-gauge round dead-soft wire
- 6 to 7 crystal 4mm bicone beads
  Note: *The bicone bead holes need to accommodate 26-gauge dead-soft wire passing through twice.*
- 1" (2.5 cm) of commercial chain

TOOLS

- Nylon-jaw wire-straightening pliers
- Flush cutters
- Chain-nose pliers
- 2/2.5 and 7/9mm bail-making pliers or round-nose pliers
- Ring mandrel
- Ruler
- Low-stick tape
- Metal file
- Silver Black or LOS, bowl, and tongs
- 0000 steel wool

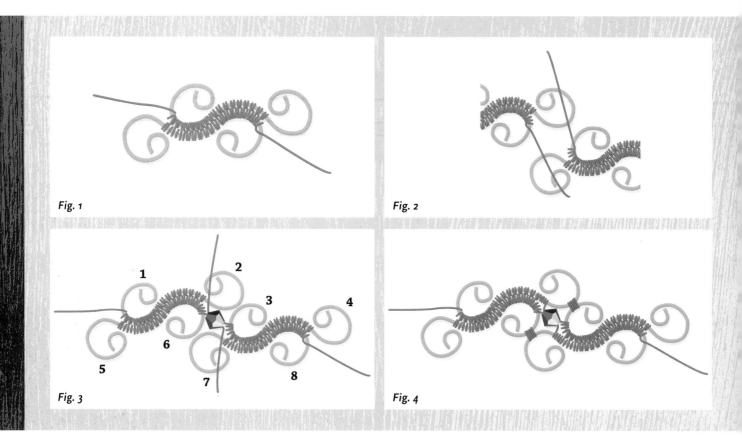

Fig. 1

Fig. 2

Fig. 3

Fig. 4

1. Make an Elegant Elle Hook using 3" (7.6 cm) of 18-gauge dead-soft wire and an Elegant Elle Eye using 2⅝" (6.7 cm) of 18-gauge dead-soft wire.

2. Make two Regal Scrolls using 2¾" (7 cm) of 18-gauge square dead-soft wire each. Follow the Regal Shape instructions to weave the Regal Scrolls together, using 24" (61 cm) of 26-gauge round dead-soft wire. Leave a 6" (15.2 cm) beginning wire tail and weave from one outside loop to the second outside loop, ending the weave on both inside loops. Do not cut the wire tails (**figure 1**).

3. Repeat Step 2, then work through Step 7 to connect the two Regal Shapes together.

4. To connect the Regal Shapes together, coil a wire tail a total of three to four times around the arch on one Regal Shape loop. Repeat this action on the diagonal arch on the second Regal Shape (**figure 2**).

5. String a 4mm bicone bead onto one coiled wire tail, then thread the second coiled wire tail through the opposite end of the bicone bead so the wires cross inside the bead. Pull the wire tails so the bicone bead is centered in between the two Regal Shapes (**figure 3**).

   Note: *In Steps 6–9, refer to this illustration for the numbering sequence of the loops that are being coiled together.*

6. Coil one wire tail one time around Loop 2, coiling toward the weave. Repeat this action with the second wire tail, coiling around Loop 7. Work back and forth, coiling each wire tail a total of three to four times. Working back and forth helps you avoid pulling the wire too tightly. Cut the wire tails.

7. With 12" (30.5 cm) of 26-gauge round dead-soft wire, coil Loop 2 to Loop 3 six to seven times, connecting the loops together. Cut the wire tails. With the remaining wire, coil Loop 6 to Loop 7 and cut the wire tails (**figure 4**).

8. Measure the length of the two woven Regal Shapes. Repeat Step 2 to make the appropriate number of sets according to your desired bracelet length, being sure to add in the length of your Elegant Elle Hook and Elegant Elle Eye when you calculate how many sets to make. With the addition of woven Regal Shapes along with your Elegant Elle Hook and Elegant Elle Eye, you may not have the exact length needed for your bracelet. However, you can use a chain extender to achieve the desired length.

9. Repeat Steps 4–7 until all the Regal Shapes are coiled together.

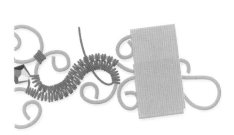

Fig. 5

Fig. 6

Fig. 7

10. To add the Elegant Elle Hook, first coil the bottom arch of the end Regal Shape with the 26-gauge round dead-soft wire tail two to three times. Hold the Elegant Elle Hook next to the Regal Shape to ensure that the coiling wire is next to the base loop on the Elegant Elle Hook. If needed, add more coils. Tape the Elegant Elle Hook to the bracelet.

    Note: *The base loop on the Elegant Elle Hook can be opened like a jump ring, so that there's room to coil* **(figure 5)**.

11. Coil the arch of the Regal Shape and base loop on the Elegant Elle Hook together five to six times. Cut the wire tail **(figure 6)**.

12. Remove the tape. With 6" (15.2 cm) of 26-gauge round dead-soft wire, coil the arch of the top Regal Shape to the curve of the Elegant Elle Hook five to six times. Cut the wire tails **(figure 7)**.

13. Repeat Steps 10–12 on the other end of the bracelet to attach the Elegant Elle Eye.

14. To make a chain extender, slide a bicone bead onto a head pin and make a wrapped loop, but before you wrap the loop closed, slide the loop through the end of the 1" (2.5 cm) chain, then wrap the loop closed. Attach the chain to the 5 mm loop of the Elegant Elle Eye.

15. The bracelet is best formed by hand. Hold each Regal Shape set between your thumbs and index fingers and curve the center of the shapes. The bracelet will be a little springy so once the bracelet is shaped, hook the bracelet shut so it retains it shape when it isn't being worn. The coils may shift slightly when you shape the bracelet. Check for any sharp edges and push them down or file them as needed.

Christy's Earrings

Throughout the writing of this book, I had the idea of creating a three-dimensional project in the back of my mind. When I started work on this design, I focused on a heart theme, but I soon realized that shaping the flat design around a mandrel would take it to the next level. My friend Christy was going through a tough time while I was working on this design. These are for her.

Techniques

◊ *Heart with modified Regal Loops (page 23)*
◊ *Scroll (page 23)*
◊ *Coiling (page 28)*
◊ *Jump Rings (optional; page 18)*
◊ *Ear Wires (page 27)*

Finished Measurement

2¼" (5.7 cm), including the ear wire

Project Notes

The filigree piece is shaped around a mandrel. I chose ParaWire's 21-gauge antique copper dead-soft wire because it's easier to curve around the mandrels than sterling silver dead-soft wire.

MATERIALS

• 32" (81.3 cm) of 21-gauge square dead-soft wire
• 6'–7' (1.8–2.1 m) of 26-gauge round dead-soft wire
• 4½" (11.4 cm) of 20-gauge round half-hard wire (ear wires)
• 6 round 20-gauge 3mm jump rings, store-bought or handmade

TOOLS

• Nylon-jaw wire-straightening pliers
• Flush cutters
• 2/2.5, 3/5 and 7/9mm bail-making pliers or round-nose pliers
• Chain-nose pliers
• Flat-nose pliers
• Ring mandrel
• Ruler
• Low-stick tape

Fig. 1

Fig. 2

Fig. 3

1. *Heart shapes:* Straighten and flush-cut four pieces of 21-gauge square dead-soft wire to 2" (5.1 cm) lengths. With a permanent marker, mark the center of each piece of wire.

2. With 5mm bail-making or round-nose pliers, make a loop on each wire end with the loops on the same side of the wire. Next, follow Step 2 only of the Regal Loop instructions (page 17), using 2mm bail-making or round-nose pliers. Repeat this step on the remaining three pieces of wire.

3. Holding the loops between your fingers, twist the wire one full time around until both loops are again on the same side of the wire. Repeat this step on one more piece of wire so there are a total of two twisted pieces of wire and two pieces not twisted.

4. With flat-nose pliers, bend the wire on the permanent-marker mark until the loops touch, creating a Heart. Repeat this step on the remaining three pieces of wire *(figure 1)*.

5. *Twisted Scrolls:* Straighten and flush-cut four 1⅞" (4.8 cm) pieces of 21-gauge square dead-soft wire. With 5mm bail-making or round-nose pliers, make a loop on one wire end. Next, follow Step 2 only of the Regal Loop instructions, using 2mm bail-making or round-nose pliers. Repeat this step on the remaining three pieces of wire.

6. On the second wire end, with 2.5mm bail-making or round-nose pliers, make a loop on the opposite side of the wire from the loop made in Step 5, creating a Scroll. Repeat this step on the remaining three pieces of wire.

7. Holding the loops between your fingers, twist the wire one full time around until the loops are again on opposite sides of the wire. Repeat this step on the remaining three Scrolls.

8. Lay the filigree pieces on a flat surface as shown in the illustration to make sure all pieces touch *(figure 2)*. If the Scrolls are too long, roll the 2.5 mm loops slightly, rolling one loop on each Scroll equally. If the Scrolls are too short, unroll the loops slightly, unrolling one loop on each Scroll equally. The scrolled ends can also be rolled or unrolled as necessary.

9. With 12" (30.5 cm) of 26-gauge round dead-soft wire, coil the two small loops of a Heart together three to four times. Cut the wire tails. Repeat this on the remaining three Heart shapes *(figure 3)*.

10. Tape together the two Heart shapes that aren't twisted, arch to arch, with one arch of each Heart shape exposed. With the remaining 26-gauge round dead-soft wire, coil the two arches together. Cut the wire tails.

    Note: Cut an additional 12" (30.5 cm) of 26-gauge wire as needed for coiling.

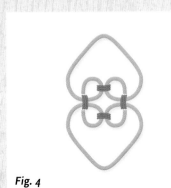

Fig. 4

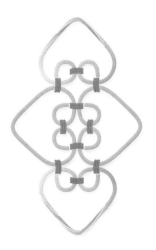

Fig. 5

11. Remove the tape and with the remaining 26-gauge round dead-soft wire, coil the second two arches together three to four times. Cut the wire tails *(figure 4)*.

12. Next, tape the arches of a twisted wire Heart shape to the center of the two coiled Heart shapes from Step 11, with one arch of the twisted Heart shape exposed. With 26-gauge round dead-soft wire, coil the two arches together three to four times. Cut the wire tails.

13. Remove the tape and with 26-gauge round dead-soft wire, coil the second two arches together three to four times. Cut the wire tails.

14. Repeat Steps 12 and 13 with the second twisted wire Heart *(figure 5)*.

15. Tape a Scroll to the Heart shapes, leaving the Regal Loop exposed. The Regal Loop should be facing the Heart shapes. With 26-gauge round dead-soft wire, coil the Regal Loop to the Heart three to four times. Cut the wire tails.

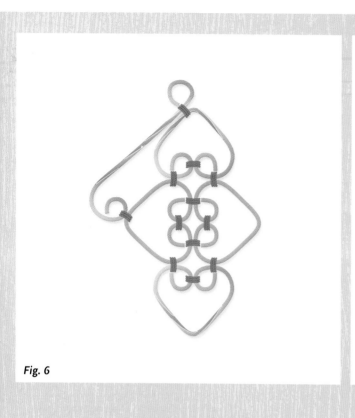

Fig. 6

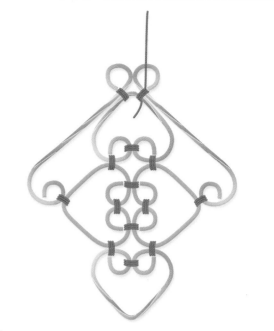

Fig. 7

16. Remove the tape, and with 26-gauge round dead-soft wire, coil the 2.5 mm loop to the Heart shape three to four times. Cut the wire tails *(figure 6)*.

17. Repeat Step 15, taping a second Scroll to the other side of the Hearts.

18. Repeat Step 16 but do not cut the wire. Instead, bring the wire up inside the 2.5 mm loop *(figure 7)*.

19. Coil the two 2.5mm Scroll loops together three to four times with the wire from Step 18. Cut the wire tails.

20. Repeat Step 15 with the third Scroll, placing the ends of the Regal Loops next to each other, but do not cut the wire. Instead, bring the wire up inside the 2 mm loop of the Regal Loop, then coil the two small loops of the Regal Loops together three to four times. Cut the wire tails.

21. Repeat Step 16.

22. Repeat Step 20 with the fourth Scroll.

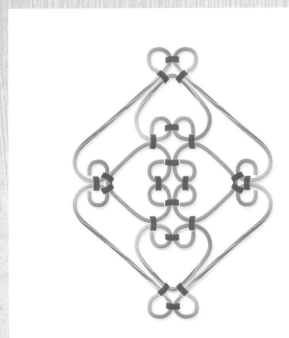

Fig. 8

Fig. 9

23. Repeat Steps 18 and 19 *(figure 8)*.

24. *Shaping:* On size 15 of a ring mandrel, shape the filigree around the mandrel with your hands, being sure to hold the center of the filigree firmly against the mandrel. Continue shaping the filigree, gradually working your way up the mandrel to size 1. Finish shaping the filigree on a 9mm mandrel (or 9mm bail-making pliers) by holding the center of the piece against the mandrel and pushing the Regal Looped sides together.

25. With 26-gauge round dead-soft wire, coil the two Regal Loops that are touching together three to four times. Cut the wire tails and repeat this step on the second two Regal Loops. Slide the earring on the 9mm mandrel one last time for shaping *(figure 9)*.

26. Attach a 3mm jump ring to each 2.5 mm loop at the top of the earring. Next, attach a 3mm jump ring through both of these jump rings.

27. Repeat Steps 1–26 for the second earring.

28. Using 4½" (11.4 cm) of 20-gauge round half-hard wire, make two ear wires. Attach the last 3mm jump ring added in Step 26 to the loop on each ear wire.

Becky's Pendant

Regal Loops create a circular frame to highlight a beautiful amethyst briolette. Amethyst dangles complete the design. Why not make matching earrings with amethysts or a set of pendant and earrings with your favorite semiprecious stones? Thanks to my friend Becky of Silver Silk for the amazing chain!

Techniques
◊ *Regal Loop (page 17)*
◊ *Coiling (page 28)*
◊ *Adding a Bead (page 28)*
◊ *Jump Rings (optional; page 18)*
◊ *Elegant Elle Hook (page 26)*
◊ *Elegant Elle Eye (page 27)*

Finished Measurements
Pendant: 1⅞" (4.8 cm); **chain and clasp:** 21½" (54.6 cm)

Project Notes
For this project, I used 18-gauge square and round sterling silver dead-soft wire and 26-gauge round sterling silver dead-soft wire. I made my Regal Loops with 5mm and 2mm bail-making pliers. The beautiful amethyst briolette and rondelles are from Rocky's Designs. I also used sterling silver round beads.

PENDANT MATERIALS
- 7½" (19.1 cm) of 18-gauge round dead-soft wire
- 5½" (14 cm) of 18-gauge square dead-soft wire
- 4' (1.2 m) of 26-gauge round dead-soft wire
- 1 semiprecious 12mm round briolette
- 2 round 3mm beads
- 6 semiprecious 3mm rondelle beads
- 6 2" (5.1 m) head pins
- 1 round 20-gauge 4mm jump ring, store-bought or handmade
- 4 round 18-gauge 7mm jump rings, store-bought or handmade

CHAIN MATERIALS
- 6" (15.2 cm) of 18-gauge round dead-soft wire
- Silver Silk 3 mm Capture Chain
- Silver Silk Capture Findings

TOOLS
- Nylon-jaw wire-straightening pliers
- Flush cutters
- 2/2.5, 3/5 and 7/9mm bail-making pliers or round-nose pliers
- Chain-nose pliers
- Flat-nose pliers
- Ring mandrel
- Ruler
- Permanent marker
- Low-stick tape

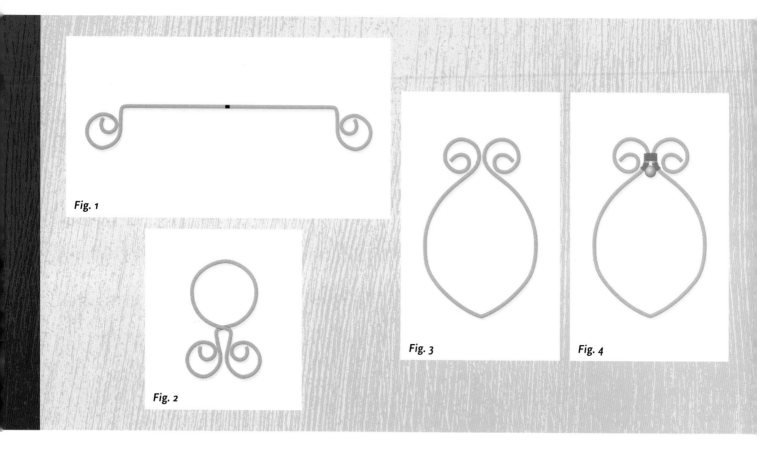

Fig. 1

Fig. 2

Fig. 3

Fig. 4

1. **Centerpiece:** Straighten and flush-cut 4½" (11.4 cm) of 18-gauge round dead-soft wire. With a permanent marker, mark the center of the wire.

2. Make Regal Loops on each wire end with 5mm and 2mm bail-making or round-nose pliers, with the loops on the same side of the wire.

3. Hold the wire with the tip of the chain-nose pliers against a Regal Loop and make a 90-degree bend. Repeat this on the second Regal Loop **(figure 1)**.

4. Hold the center mark on the wire against size 1 on a ring mandrel with the top of the Regal Loops facing toward the mandrel. Shape the wire around the mandrel, crossing the Regal Loops. Remove from the ring mandrel and remove the permanent marker mark. Set aside **(figure 2)**.

5. **Outside Frame:** Straighten and flush-cut 5½" (14 cm) of 18-gauge square dead-soft wire. Mark the center with a permanent marker. With flat-nose pliers, make a bend on the mark, creating a wide V.

6. Make Regal Loops on each wire end with 5mm and 2mm bail-making or round-nose pliers, with the loops going toward the outside of the V.

7. Hold the bend against size 15 on a ring mandrel and shape the wire around the mandrel until the Regal Loops touch. Remove from the ring mandrel and remove the permanent marker mark **(figure 3)**.

8. With 12" (30.5 cm) of 26-gauge round dead-soft wire, coil the Regal Loops together three to four times, then add a 3mm round bead. Cut the wire tails **(figure 4)**.

9. Place the centerpiece inside the outside frame to check the size. If the centerpiece is too large, roll the Regal Loops equally, making the centerpiece smaller.

10. Remove the centerpiece from the outside frame. With the remaining 26-gauge round dead-soft wire from Step 8, coil the Regal Loops of the centerpiece together three to four times, then add a 3mm round bead. Cut the wire tails **(figure 5)**.
    Note: Cut additional 12" (30.5 cm) pieces of 26-gauge round dead-soft wire as needed.

11. Tape the centerpiece inside the outside frame, taping across the middle of the two pieces. With the remaining 26-gauge round dead-soft wire from Step 10, coil each Regal Loop of the centerpiece to the outside frame three to four times. Cut the wire tails **(figure 6)**.

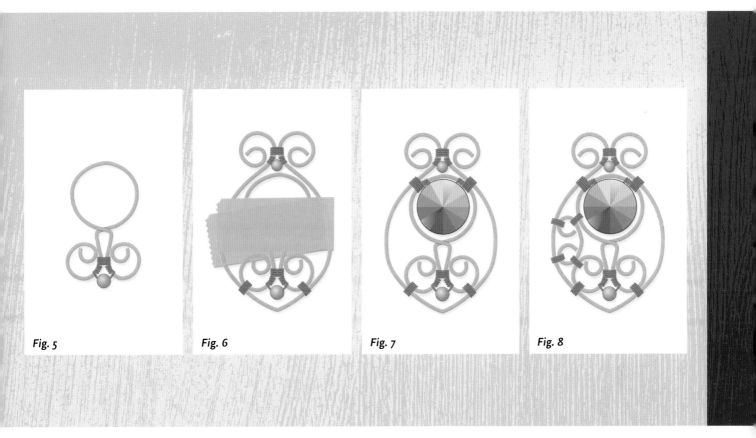

Fig. 5 Fig. 6 Fig. 7 Fig. 8

12. With 12" (30.5 cm) of 26-gauge round dead-soft wire and coiling toward the top of the piece, coil the left side of the centerpiece to the outside frame four to five times. Remove the tape, then add the 12mm briolette. Cut the wire tails *(figure 7)*.

13. *Side Pieces:* Flush-cut 1⅛" (2.9 cm) of 18-gauge round dead-soft wire. With 2.5mm bail-making or round-nose pliers, make a loop on each wire end with the loops on the same side of the wire. With 2mm bail-making or round-nose pliers, hold the center of the wire in between the two loops and shape the loops around the pliers. Repeat this step, creating a second side piece.

14. Set the pieces inside the frame with the loops facing outward. If the pieces are too big, equally roll the loops more until they fit alongside the centerpiece.

15. Tape one side piece in place, leaving the bottom loop exposed.

16. With 26-gauge wire, coil the bottom loop to the outside frame three to four times. Cut the wire tails. Next, coil the bottom loop to the Regal Loop on the centerpiece three to four times. Cut the wire tails.

17. Repeat Step 16, coiling the top loop to the outside frame and then coil the top loop to the large centerpiece loop *(figure 8)*.

18. Repeat Steps 15–17 for the second side piece.

19. Slide a 3mm rondelle onto a head pin. Make a wrapped loop and cut the head pin tail. Repeat this five times for a total of six.

20. Open a 4mm jump ring and hook it around the bottom tip of the outside frame. Slide the six wrapped rondelles onto the jump ring then close the jump ring.

21. Make an Elegant Elle Hook using 3" (7.6 cm) of 18-gauge round dead-soft wire and an Elegant Elle Eye using 2⅝" (6.7 cm) of 18-gauge round dead-soft wire.

22. Attach two 7mm jump rings to each Regal Loop at the top of the pendant. Cut the chain to desired length then slide the chain through the four jump rings. Attach the findings to the chain ends then attach the Elegant Elle Hook and Elegant Elle Eye to the findings.

Lisa's Ring

I really wanted to design a ring for this book, but I was having trouble coming up with an idea. While I was creating Misti's Bracelet (page 52), I noticed how nicely the ends of the Regal Shapes fit together with the bicone beads and thought, "That's it! A ring!" I liked the idea so much, I made two—one with silver wire and a red Swarovski crystal bicone bead and one with copper and a purple bicone bead.

Techniques
◊ *Regal Scroll (page 24)*
◊ *Regal Shape (page 25)*
◊ *Coiling (page 28)*
◊ *Weave Pattern (page 29)*

Finished Size
Size 5½

Project Notes
The Regal Shape is made up of two Regal Scrolls woven together. I used 18-gauge round copper dead-soft wire for this ring, with a 4mm bicone bead. For the variation, I used 18-gauge round dead-soft sterling silver with a 6 mm bicone bead. For this ring, I used 5mm bail-making pliers for the large loop and 2mm for the small loop. My finished ring size is 5½. The instructions explain how to change the ring size.

RING MATERIALS
- 4" (10.2 cm) of 18-gauge round dead-soft scrap wire
- 8"–10" (20.3–25.4 cm) of 18-gauge round dead-soft wire
- 5'–6' (1.5–1.8 m) of 26-gauge round dead-soft wire
- 1 crystal or glass 4mm bicone bead
  Note: *The bicone bead hole needs to accommodate 26-gauge round dead-soft wire passing through twice.*

TOOLS
- Nylon-jaw wire-straightening pliers
- Flush cutters
- Ring mandrel
- 2/2.5 and 3/5mm bail-making pliers or round-nose pliers
- Ruler
- Low-stick tape

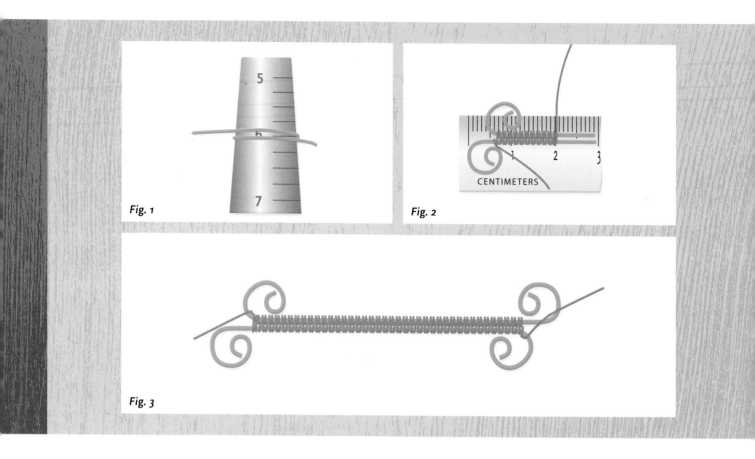

Fig. 1

Fig. 2

Fig. 3

1. To calculate how much wire you need for your desired ring size, you'll need to do some math. This example is based on a final ring size of 5½. Because of the displacement caused by weaving and having to angle the ring when it's shaped, Step 1 should be calculated at one-half size larger than your final desired ring size. For this example's final ring size of 5½, I'm sizing the wire at ring size 6.

   Cut 4" (10.2 cm) of 18-gauge round dead-soft scrap wire. Wrap the wire around a ring mandrel at size 5½ or your final desired ring size, pulling the wire tightly. The wire ends need to cross. When the wire ends are released, because of spring-back in the wire, the wire should rest on size 6 or one-half size larger than your desired ring size. If it doesn't, slide the wire up to size 5¼ or one-quarter smaller than your desired ring size and pull the wire ends. Release the wire again to check the size. Repeat as necessary until the wire rests at size 6 or one-half size larger than your desired ring size *(figure 1)*.

   Flush-cut both wire ends at any spot where they overlap, then slide the wire back on the ring mandrel to check the sizing again, ensuring it is size 6, or ½ size larger than your required size.

   When the size has been verified, straighten the wire and measure the length. Make note of this length. My size 6 wire measures 2³⁄₁₆" (5.6 cm).

2. To make the large loop on one end of a Regal Scroll with 5mm bail-making pliers and ⅛" (3.2 mm) over-roll takes 1⅛" (2.9 cm). Because you'll be making two loops on each Regal Scroll, you'll need 1⅛" (2.9 cm) × 2 = 2¼" (5.7 cm) of wire. Add this number to the number in Step 1: 2³⁄₁₆" (5.6 cm) + 2¼" (5.7 cm) = 4⁷⁄₁₆" (11.3 cm).

3. If you make the large Regal Scroll loop with 5mm bail-making pliers, the width of the loop should be ⁵⁄₁₆" (7.9 mm) × 2 (because there are 2 loops on each Scroll) = ¹⁰⁄₁₆" (1.6 cm). Subtract this amount from the total in Step 2: 4⁷⁄₁₆" (11.3 cm) – ¹⁰⁄₁₆" (1.6 cm) = 3¹³⁄₁₆" (9.7 cm). This is the total length of wire needed for one Regal Scroll. Because you need two Regal Scrolls to make the Regal Shape, multiply by two: 3¹³⁄₁₆" (9.7 cm) × 2 = 7¹⁰⁄₁₆" or 7⅝" (19.4 cm) of 18-gauge round dead-soft wire is needed to make this Regal Shape ring.

4. Cut 7⅝" (19.4 cm), or whatever length you calculated, of 18-gauge round dead-soft wire, then cut that in half. Make two Regal Scrolls using 5mm bail-making pliers to make the large (5 mm) loops, with a ⅛" (3.2 mm) over-roll. If you measure the Regal Scrolls now, each should measure 2³⁄₁₆" (5.6 cm) or your measurement from Step 1. If the wires are too long or short, over-roll or unroll each loop until the required length is achieved before making the 2 mm loops. Complete the Regal Scrolls following Steps 3–5 of Regal Scrolls in the Essential Techniques chapter.

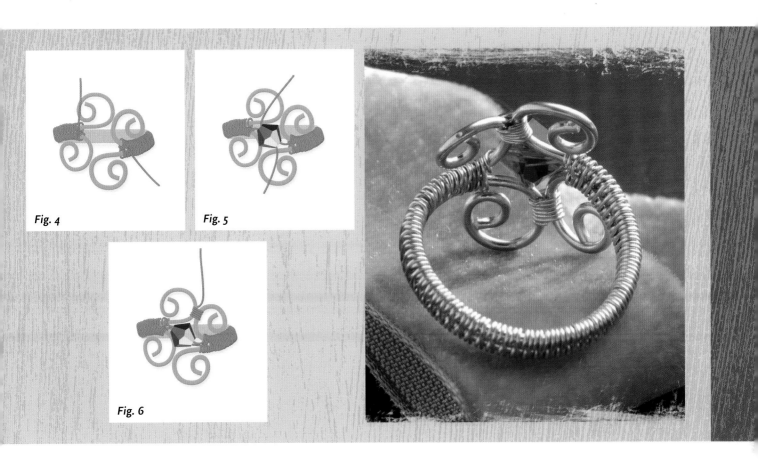

Fig. 4

Fig. 5

Fig. 6

5. With 4' (1.2 m) of 26-gauge round dead-soft wire and leaving an 8" (20.3 cm) beginning wire tail, follow the Weave Pattern to weave the two Regal Scrolls together. Weave approximately ½" (1.3 cm). Holding the weave, gently pull the Regal Scrolls until the weave is positioned at one end of the halves, offsetting the loops by the bead size, 4mm. Measure from the outside of one loop to the outside of the second loop *(figure 2)*.

Note: *To use a larger bead, offset the loops by that bead size. When making a larger size ring, cut a longer piece of 26-gauge round dead-soft wire.*

6. Continue weaving to the curve of the shorter loop, then coil once around the shorter loop. As you weave, periodically check the offset measurement to ensure that your Regal Scrolls haven't shifted. Do not cut the wire tail *(figure 3)*.

7. With the beginning wire tail, weave to the curve of the shorter loop, then coil once around the shorter loop, as in Step 6.

8. Shape the ring on the ring mandrel. Because of wire spring-back, you may need to shape the ring at a smaller size than your desired size. When the ring is removed from the mandrel, the loops are horizontal to each other, but they need to be at an angle to each other. Angle the loops by holding the ring shank on each side of the loops and pushing one side of the ring up and the second side of the ring down *(figure 4)*.

9. Thread each wire end through the 4mm bicone bead in opposite directions so the wires cross inside the bead.

10. Pull each wire end until the bicone bead sits in between the Regal Scroll loops. Angle the bead so the bead hole is in between the loops *(figure 5)*.

11. Coil one wire tail one time around the curve of a loop, coiling toward the weave.

12. Repeat Step 11 with the second wire tail. Cut both wire tails.

13. With 8" (20.3 cm) of 26-gauge round dead-soft wire, coil the curve of two loops together five to six times *(figure 6)*. Cut the wire tails.

14. Repeat Step 13 on the second two loops. The bead will sit low, toward the inside of the ring shank. When you size the ring, continue to push the ring down on the mandrel to your final desired size. Doing so will push the bead up, making it level with the shank.

Kathy's Bracelet

Scrolls, scrolls, scrolls—I can't get enough of them. Silver scrolls wind their way around the band and frame one of Kathy Hoppe's (of O'Gosh Buttons & Beads) beautiful lampwork beads.

Techniques
◊ *Elegant Elle Hook (page 26)*
◊ *Scroll (page 23)*
◊ *Coiling (page 28)*
◊ *Jump Rings (optional; page 18)*

Finished Measurement
7½" (19.1 cm)

Project Notes
I used 18-gauge square sterling silver dead-soft wire with 26-gauge round dead-soft wire to make the bracelet and add bicones in between the Scrolls. Bicones can be replaced with your favorite 4mm beads. Beads surrounding the focal bead need to fit in the space between the focal bead and the wire frame.

MATERIALS
- 38"–40" (96.5 cm–1 m) 18-gauge square dead-soft wire
- 11'–12' (3.4–3.7 m) of 26-gauge round dead-soft wire
- 1 lampwork 23mm × 19mm bicone bead (focal bead)
- 6 crystal 4mm bicone beads
  Note: *The bead holes need to accommodate 26-gauge wire passing through twice.*
- 2 round 5mm 20-gauge jump rings, store-bought or handmade
- 2 round 7mm 18-gauge jump rings, store-bought or handmade

TOOLS
- Nylon-jaw wire-straightening pliers
- Flush cutters
- Chain-nose pliers
- Flat-nose pliers
- 2/2.5, 3/5 and 7/9mm bail-making pliers or round-nose pliers
- Ruler
- Low-stick tape
- Permanent marker
- Gridded composition paper
- Nylon-jaw bracelet-forming pliers or bracelet mandrel

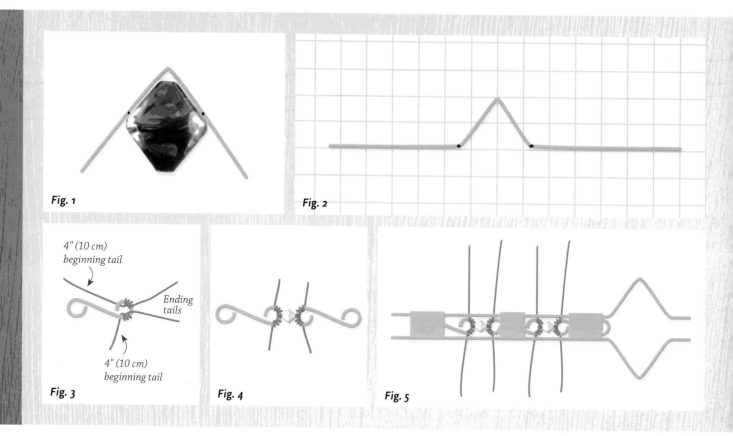

Fig. 1

Fig. 2

4" (10 cm)
beginning tail

Ending
tails

4" (10 cm)
beginning tail

Fig. 3

Fig. 4

Fig. 5

1. Make an Elegant Elle Hook using 3" (7.6 cm) of 18-gauge square dead-soft wire.

2. Straighten and cut two 9" (22.9 cm) pieces of 18-gauge square dead soft wire (these are the frames for the bracelet). With a permanent marker, mark the center of both pieces.

3. With flat-nose pliers, make a bend on the center mark, creating a V, so the wire outlines half of the bead. Repeat this on the second piece of wire.

4. Holding one wire against the bead, mark each side of the wire 2 mm higher than the middle of the bead *(figure 1)*.

5. With flat-nose pliers, make a bend on each mark so the wire runs lengthwise to the bead. Check the bends and straightness of your wire on gridded composition paper *(figure 2)*.

6. Repeat Steps 4 and 5 on the second piece of wire. Remove the permanent marker marks from both pieces of wire.

7. Straighten and flush-cut six 1⅜" (3.5 cm) pieces of 18-gauge square dead-soft wire. Using 3mm bail-making pliers or round-nose pliers, make six Scrolls.

8. Cut two 9" (22.9 cm) pieces of 26-gauge round dead-soft wire. Leaving a 4" (10.2 cm) beginning tail, coil a Scroll loop three times, with the beginning tail being under the loop and the ending tail being on top of the loop. The ending tail needs to be in the center of the loop. Repeat this with the second 9" (22.9 cm) piece of wire *(figure 3)*.

9. Slide a 4mm bead onto both ending wire tails, then coil each tail around a Scroll loop on a second Scroll three times, starting in the center of the loop. The ending tails should be on the bottom of the loops when coiling is completed. Do not cut any wire tails *(figure 4)*.

10. Repeat Steps 8 and 9, adding a second bicone and third Scroll. This group of three Scrolls/two bicones is for one side of the bracelet. Set aside.

11. Repeat Steps 8–10, making a second group of Scrolls and bicone beads for the second side of the bracelet.

12. Pull the 26-gauge round dead-soft wire tails at a 90-degree angle to the Scrolls. Line up one of the Scroll loops at the bends of the frame wires, with the wire tails as shown, then tape the pieces together *(figure 5)*.

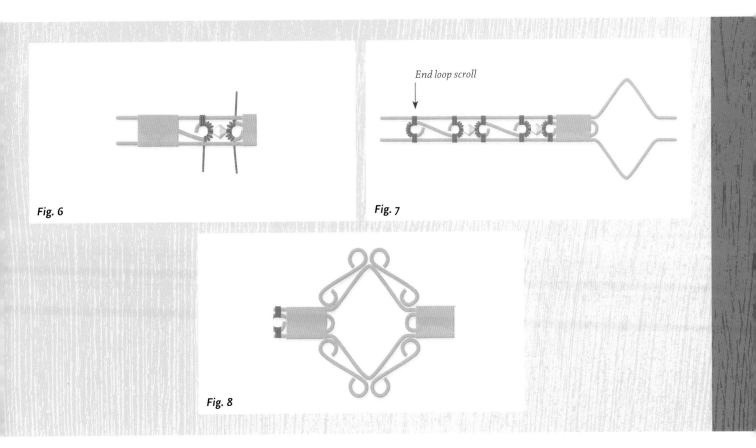

Fig. 6

Fig. 7

End loop scroll

Fig. 8

13. With a wire tail, coil a Scroll loop to the frame wire three times, then cut the wire tail. Repeat this seven times, coiling all of the wire tails to the frames **(figure 6)**.

14. Remove all tape except the tape around the Scroll next to the center of the frame bends. With 8" (20.3 cm) of 26-gauge dead-soft wire, coil the end Scroll loop to the frame wire three times. Coil the Scroll loop eight times, then coil the loop to the second frame wire three times. Cut the wire tails. The Scroll loop next to the center of the frame bends will be coiled in Steps 19–20 **(figure 7)**.

15. Repeat Steps 12–14 on the second group of Scrolls/bicones.
Note: *If you're using sterling silver to construct your bracelet, Step 16 should first be done with copper to determine the length of wire needed to make your Scrolls.*

16. Straighten and flush-cut four 1⁷⁄₁₆" (3.7 cm) pieces of 18-gauge square dead-soft wire or your required length to make Scrolls that will fit the outside of your frame. Your required length may vary, depending on the location of the bends you made in Step 4. Using 3mm bail-making pliers or round-nose pliers, make four Scrolls. Lay the Scrolls next to the center top and bottom of the frame wires, ensuring the tops of the Scrolls touch and the bottom of the Scrolls touch the bracelet frame **(figure 8)**.

17. With 5" (12.7 cm) of 26-gauge round dead-soft wire, coil the top two Scroll loops together three times, then coil the bottom two Scroll loops together three times. Do not cut the wire tails because the coil can loosen while the piece is being attached to the bracelet. If the tails are intact, you can easily tighten them in a later step before cutting.

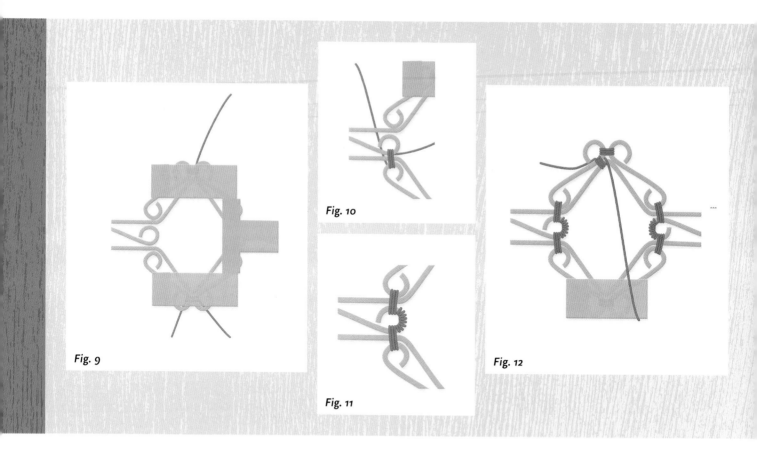

Fig. 9

Fig. 10

Fig. 11

Fig. 12

18. Tape the Scrolls to the top and bottom of the frame wires, leaving one side of the lengthwise Scrolls exposed **(figure 9)**.

19. With 8" (20.3 cm) of 26-gauge round dead-soft wire, coil the bottom Scroll loop to the center Scroll loop three times. Bring the wire tail up inside the center of the bracelet frame **(figure 10)**.

20. Coil the center Scroll loop eight times, then coil the center Scroll loop to the loop of the top Scroll three times. Cut both wire tails **(figure 11)**.

21. Remove the tape from the second side of the bracelet, then repeat Steps 19 and 20 on that side of the bracelet.

22. Tighten and cut the 26-gauge round dead-soft wire tails of the top two Scroll loops (from Step 17). With 7" (17.8 cm) of 26-gauge round dead-soft wire, coil the top left Scroll loop to the frame three times, coiling toward the top of the piece. Bring the wire up between the Scroll and the center point of the bracelet frame **(figure 12)**.

23. With 7" (17.8 cm) of 26-gauge dead-soft wire coil the top right Scroll loop to the frame three times, bringing the wire up between the Scroll and the center point of the bracelet frame.

    Note: *Hold the frame upside down to coil from right to left.*

24. Remove the tape from the bottom Scrolls, then tighten and cut the 26-gauge wire tails of the bottom two Scroll loops (from Step 17).

Fig. 13

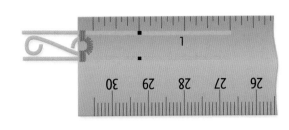

Fig. 14

Fig. 15

25. String a 4mm bicone, the focal bead, and a second 4mm bicone onto both 26-gauge round dead-soft wire ends. Thread one 26-gauge wire between the Scroll and the center point of the frame on the bottom, then coil around one Scroll loop three times *(figure 13)*.

26. Thread the second 26-gauge round dead-soft wire between the Scroll and the center point of the frame, then coil the wire around the second bottom Scroll loop three times. Cut the four 26-gauge round dead-soft wire tails.

27. To finish the bracelet ends, measure ½" (1.3 cm) from the outside of the end Scroll, marking both frame wires at ½" (1.3 cm) *(figure 14)*.

28. Flush-cut both frame wires on the mark. With 2mm bail-making pliers, make loops on each wire end, with the loops facing out from the center of the bracelet. With your fingers, push the two loops together.

29. With 8" (20.3 cm) of 26-gauge round dead-soft wire, coil the loops together four times. Cut the wire tails *(figure 15)*.

30. Repeat Steps 27–29 on the second side of the bracelet, using the remaining 26-gauge round dead-soft wire from Step 29 to coil the loops together.

Variation

To make your bracelet longer or shorter, vary the lengths of the Scrolls, add or subtract Scrolls, or use a chain extender (see Step 16 of Charli's Bracelet, page 103). You can also make the band of your bracelet wider by making larger Scrolls (for example, 5 mm loops instead of 3 mm loops).

31. Attach one 5mm jump ring to each loop at one end of the bracelet, then attach the jump rings to the base loop of the Elegant Elle Hook.

32. Attach two 7mm jump rings to the two end loops on the second side of the bracelet for the hook to latch through.

33. Shape the bracelet with nylon-jaw bracelet-forming pliers or on a bracelet mandrel.

DeeDee's Bracelet

Two hearts are better than one in this lovely linked bracelet. Heart shapes framed with twisted wire alternate with paired Regal Loops, which combine to create a second heart motif. Thank you, DeeDee, for introducing me to Whim-Z Wire. *I love it!*

Techniques

◊ *Elegant Elle Hook (page 26)*
◊ *Scroll (page 23)*
◊ *Regal Loop (page 17)*
◊ *Coiling (page 28)*
◊ *Heart (page 23)*
◊ *Adding a Bead (modified; page 28)*
◊ *Jump Rings (optional; page 18)*
◊ *Wrapped Loop (optional; page 16)*

Finished Measurement

7" (17.8 cm) including the clasp

Project Notes

When I was designing this bracelet, I came up with the idea of Regal Loops for the first time. Their identical Scrolls complement the Heart shapes. The Scrolls are controlled, while the Heart-shape arches are freehand. I used 18-gauge twisted copper dead-soft Whim-Z wire, 21-gauge half-round dead-soft ParaWire, and 26-gauge round dead-soft wire.

MATERIALS

- 23" (58.4 cm) of 18-gauge square dead-soft wire
- 30" (76.2 cm) of 18-gauge twisted dead-soft wire
- 5–6' (1.5–1.8 m) of 21-gauge half-round dead-soft wire
- 12"–24" (30.5–61 cm) of 26-gauge round dead-soft wire
- 3 faceted 10mm briolettes
- 20 round 18-gauge twisted 4mm jump rings, store-bought or handmade
- 2 round 18-gauge twisted 7mm jump rings, store-bought or handmade
- *Optional: 1" (2.5 cm) of commercial chain, 1 head pin, and 1 bead*

TOOLS

- Nylon-jaw wire-straightening pliers
- Flush cutters
- Chain-nose pliers
- 2/2.5, 3/5 and 7/9mm bail-making pliers or round-nose pliers
- Flat-nose pliers
- Nylon-jaw bracelet-forming pliers or bracelet mandrel
- Ruler
- Low-stick tape
- Permanent marker
- Gridded composition paper

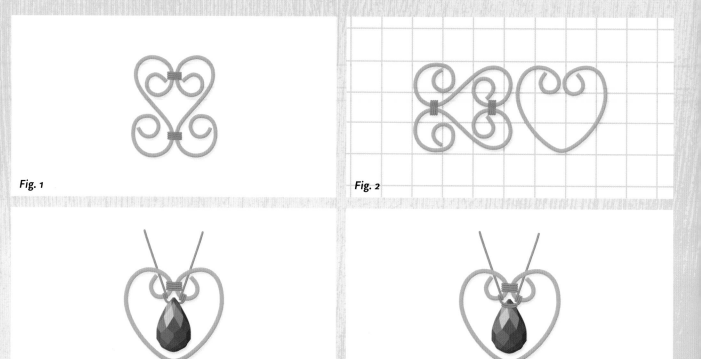

Fig. 1

Fig. 2

Fig. 3

Fig. 4

1. Make an Elegant Elle Hook using 3" (7.6 cm) of 18-gauge square dead-soft wire.

2. *Scrolls:* Straighten and flush-cut 2¾" (7 cm) of 18-gauge square dead-soft wire. Use 7mm bail-making pliers or round-nose pliers for Step 1 of Regal Loop (page 17), making a loop on each wire end with the loops on the opposite sides of the wire. For Step 2 of Regal Loops, use 2.5mm bail-making or round-nose pliers.

3. Repeat Step 2 three times for a total of four Scrolls.

4. With 12" (30.5 cm) of 26-gauge round dead-soft wire, coil the top and bottom of two Scrolls together four to five times as shown. Cut the wire tails *(figure 1)*.

5. Repeat Step 4, with the second set of Scrolls.

6. *Heart shape:* Straighten and flush-cut 3" (7.6 cm) of 18-gauge square dead-soft wire. Follow the Heart shape. For the small loops, I used 2.5mm bail-making pliers.

Repeat Step 2 of the Heart-shape instructions for a total of three heart shapes.

Note: The heart shapes need to be the same height as the set of Scrolls used to make the wire frame in Step 22. Place the pieces side by side on gridded composition paper to check the height. If necessary, adjust the Arched Loops of the Heart shape to equal the height of the set of Scrolls. It's okay if the Scrolls are longer than the Heart shape (figure 2).

7. To add a briolette to a Heart shape, the usual technique for adding a bead (page 28) will be modified. With 12" (30.5 cm) of 26-gauge round dead-soft wire, coil the two Heart-shape loops together four or five times. Cut both wire tails. With the remaining wire, coil one time around a small loop, string the briolette, then coil twice around the second small loop *(figure 3)*.

8. Pull the wire across the back of the briolette, then coil the wire around the briolette twice *(figure 4)*.

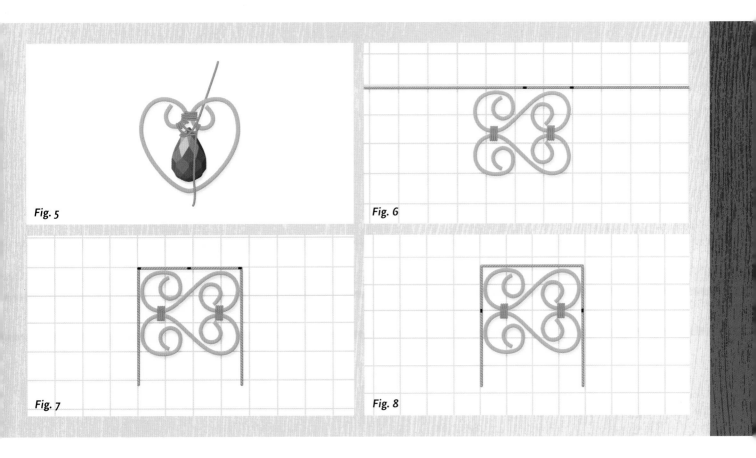

Fig. 5

Fig. 6

Fig. 7

Fig. 8

9. Hold the wire against the back of the briolette, then bend it up toward the loop where the beginning wire tail is. Thread the wire through the loop *(figure 5)*.

10. Coil the wire one time around the loop, then cut both wire tails on the back side of the briolette.

11. Repeat Steps 7–10, adding a briolette to the two remaining Heart shapes.

12. To make one-half of the wire frame for a Scrolls set, cut 3" (7.6 cm) of 18-gauge twisted dead-soft wire. Mark the center of the wire with a permanent marker.

13. Place a Scroll set sideways on gridded composition paper with the right end of the Scrolls next to the corner of a box. Center the 3" (7.6 cm) piece of 18-gauge twisted dead-soft wire over the top of the Scroll set. Mark the wire at the corner of the box *(figure 6)*.

14. With flat-nose pliers, make a 90-degree bend on the corner mark.

15. Mark the wire at the corner of the box on the left end of the Scrolls. Repeat Step 14 *(figure 7)*.

16. Next, place the middle of the Scroll set and frame on a line of the gridded composition paper. Mark each side of the frame wire on this line *(figure 8)*. Measure the distance from the corner to this mark and make note of this measurement because you'll need it in Step 22.

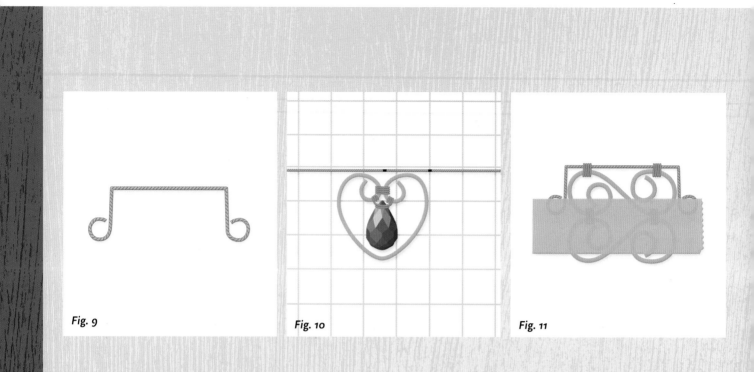

Fig. 9

Fig. 10

Fig. 11

17. Flush-cut the frame wire on each side ⁵⁄₁₆" (7.9mm) from the marks made in Step 16.

18. Using 2.5mm bail-making pliers or round-nose pliers, make a loop on each end of the frame wire, with the loops going to the outside of the frame *(figure 9)*.

19. Repeat Steps 12–18, making the second half of the frame. Rub off the permanent marker marks. Set aside the frame halves and the Scroll set.

20. Repeat Steps 12–18, making two more frame halves for the second Scroll set. Rub off the permanent marker marks. Set aside the second frame halves and Scroll sets.

21. To make the frame for a Heart shape, cut 3" (7.6 cm) of 18-gauge twisted dead-soft wire. Mark the center of the frame wire with a permanent marker. Place a Heart shape on gridded composition paper with the arches next to a line and one side of the Heart shape next to a line. Center the frame wire over the Heart-shape arches. Mark the wire at the corner of the box *(figure 10)*.

22. Repeat Steps 14–16, using the measurement from Step 16 to mark the Heart-shape frame on each side. As mentioned in Step 7, the Heart shape and Scroll sets need to be the same height for the wire frames. If the Scroll set is longer than the width of the Heart, that's okay.

23. Flush-cut the Heart-shape frame wire on each side ⁵⁄₁₆" (7.9mm) from the marks made in Step 22.

24. Repeat Steps 21–23 to make the second half of the Heart frame.

25. Repeat Steps 21–23 to make the two frame halves for the remaining two Hearts. Rub off the permanent marker marks. Set the frame halves and Heart shapes aside.

26. Tape one-half of the Scroll frame and its corresponding Scroll set together. With 12" (30.5 cm) of 21-gauge half-round dead-soft wire, coil the top of the frame and the top of the Scroll set loops three to four times. Cut the wire tails *(figure 11)*.

27. Reposition the tape as necessary. With the remaining wire, coil the sides of the frame to the sides of the Scroll set loops three to four times. Cut the wire tails.

28. Repeat Steps 26–27 to attach the second half of the frame, using the remaining 21-gauge half-round dead-soft wire. Cut additional 12" (30.5 cm) lengths as needed.

29. Using 21-gauge half-round dead-soft wire, coil the frame loops on both ends together two to three times. Cut the wire tails.

30. Repeat Steps 26–29, coiling the second Scroll frame halves to the second Scroll set.

Fig. 12

31. Repeat Steps 26–27, coiling the top arches of the Heart shape and the side of the Heart shape to a Heart-shape frame half.

32. Tape the second half of the frame and Heart shape together. Coil the bottom of the Heart shape to the frame two to three times, then repeat Step 29 (*figure 12*).

33. Repeat Steps 31 and 32, coiling the remaining Heart-shape frame halves to the other two Heart shapes.

34. Using either nylon-jaw bracelet-forming pliers or a bracelet mandrel, slightly curve the Scroll sets and Scroll frames, and the Heart shapes and Heart-shape frames.

35. Connect the Heart-shape frames with two 4mm jump rings through each loop, connecting a Heart-shape frame to a Scroll-set frame. Use two 4mm jump rings to attach the base loop of the Elegant Elle Hook to each loop at the end of a Heart-shape frame.

36. Attach a 7mm jump ring to each loop on the last Heart-shape frame for the hook to latch through.

Optional: To make a chain extender, string a bead onto a head pin and make a Wrapped Loop, but before wrapping the loop closed, slide the loop through the end of the 1" (2.5 cm) chain. Then, wrap the loop closed. Attach the chain to both 7mm jump rings on the end of the bracelet.

Variation
Change the connecting loops to the top and bottom of the frames, connect two framed Heart segments, and—voilà!—earrings.

Joanna's Bracelet

For this bracelet, four Elegant Elle shapes are coiled together to create one Elle cluster. Four clusters are then joined and accented with beautiful amazonite rondelles. I made this bracelet for my daughter Joanna, who likes girly, pretty things, and it's one of my favorites.

Techniques

◊ *Elegant Elle Hook (page 26)*
◊ *Elegant Elle (EE; page 22)*
◊ *Arched Loop (page 16)*
◊ *Coiling (page 28)*
◊ *Elegant Elle Eye (optional; page 27)*
◊ *Wrapped Loop (page 16)*
◊ *Jump Rings (optional; page 18)*

Finished Measurements

6½" (16.5 cm) plus 1½" (3.8 cm) extender

Project Notes

I used 18-gauge square sterling silver dead-soft wire for my clusters and 26-gauge round sterling silver dead-soft wire for coiling. My loops are 2 mm. I suggest making a mock-up cluster with copper or craft wire to fit the shapes together, then using this mock-up cluster as your template.

MATERIALS

- 4'–5' (1.2–1.5 m) of 18-gauge square dead-soft wire
- 7'–8' (2.1–2.4 m) of 26-gauge round dead-soft wire
- 4 round 4mm 20-gauge jump rings, store-bought or handmade
- 4–5 faceted 10mm rondelles
- 8–10 round 4mm daisy spacers
  Note: *The rondelle and daisy spacer holes need to accommodate 26-gauge dead soft wire passing through twice.*
- 1" (2.5 cm) of commercial chain
- 1 head pin

TOOLS

- Nylon-jaw wire-straightening pliers
- Flush cutters
- Chain-nose pliers
- 2/2.5 and 7/9mm bail-making pliers or round-nose pliers
- Flat-nose pliers
- Ring mandrel
- Ruler
- Low-stick tape
- Permanent marker
- Metal file

Fig. 1

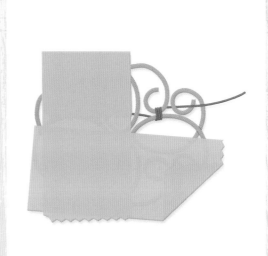

Fig. 2

1. Make an Elegant Elle Hook using 3" (7.6 cm) of 18-gauge square dead-soft wire.

   Note: *There are two different sizes of EE shapes within each cluster. The two outside EE shapes have smaller Arched Loops than the center EE shapes. This lets the four centers of each EE shape touch.*

2. Make one cluster, working through Step 12. For each cluster, straighten and flush-cut two 2¾" (7 cm) pieces of 18-gauge square dead-soft wire to make the two center EE shapes. Flush-cut two 2½" (5.6 cm) pieces of 18-gauge square dead-soft wire to make the two outside EE shapes. Follow the instructions for the EE shape (page 22), but with these differences:

   A) Skip Step 2.

   B) For Step 3, hold the center mark, as opposed to the center of the V, against the ring mandrel.

   C) For Step 4, hold the center mark with 2mm bail-making or round-nose pliers on the center mark, pushing both wire ends at the same time. Doing so makes the centers of each EE shape rounded instead of pointed, which will make it easier to fit the four centers together.

   D) In Step 5, when you make the Arched Loops for the EE shapes, leave the loops slightly open for ease of coiling the pieces together, and roll the Arched Loops on all EE shapes until they touch the center loop.

3. Lay out the EE shapes, fitting them together so the centers of the larger EE shapes touch, and the centers of the smaller EE shapes touch the centers of the larger EE shapes. If your center and Arched Loops don't touch, the Arched Loops of EE2 and EE4 can be adjusted by gently pushing the arches up or down with your fingers. In Steps 4–7, refer to this illustration for the numbering sequence of the EE shapes that are being coiled together **(figure 1)**.

4. Once the EE shapes are fitted in place, you can tape them together, leaving the Arched Loop of EE1 and the center loop and Arched Loop of EE2 exposed. With 12" (30.5 cm) of 26-gauge round dead-soft wire, coil the center loop of EE2 to the Arched Loop of EE1 three to four times. Bring the wire up in the arched loop of EE2 **(figure 2)**.

5. Coil the Arched Loops of EE1 and EE2 together three to four times. Cut the wire tails.

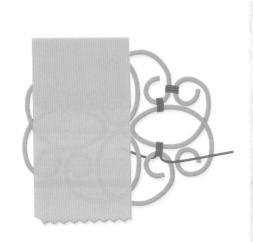

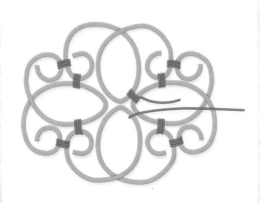

Fig. 3

Fig. 4

6. Remove and reposition the tape, exposing the center and Arched Loops of EE2 and the Arched Loop of EE3. With the remaining 26-gauge round dead-soft wire, coil the Arched Loop of EE3 to the center loop of EE2 three to four times. Bring the wire up in the Arched Loop of EE3 **(figure 3)**.

7. Coil the Arched Loops of EE2 and EE3 together three to four times. Cut the wire tails.

   Note: *Cut an additional 12" (30.5 cm) of 26-gauge round dead-soft wire as needed.*

8. To coil together the remaining EE shapes, repeat Steps 4–7. In Steps 4 and 5, coil the center loop of EE4 to the Arched Loop of EE3, then coil the Arched Loops of EE3 and EE4 together. In Steps 6 and 7, coil the Arched Loop of EE1 to the center loop of EE4, then coil the Arched Loops of EE4 and EE1 together.

9. With 6" (15.2 cm) of 26-gauge round dead-soft wire, coil the center loops of EE1 and EE2 together three to four times. Bring the wire up in the center loop of EE3 **(figure 4)**.

10. Coil the center loops of EE2 and EE3 together three to four times. Cut the wire tails.

11. Repeat Steps 9 and 10, coiling the center loops of EE3 and EE4 together, then EE1 and EE4 together.

Fig. 5

12. **Shaping the Clusters:** Curve EE2 by holding the center loops of EE1 and EE3 in between your thumb and index finger, then hold the Arched Loops of EE1, EE2 and EE3 with wire-straightening pliers (or flat-nose pliers) and gently bend the arches down. Repeat these actions on EE4 **(figure 5)**.

    Note: *Measure the length of the EE cluster. Make the appropriate number of EE-shape clusters according to your desired bracelet length, being sure to add in the length of your connecting beads and Elegant Elle Hook. Your clusters, beads, and Elegant Elle Hook may not be the exact desired length for your bracelet. Because of this, a chain extender can be used, smaller or larger beads can be used in between the EE clusters, or an Elegant Elle Eye for the Elegant Elle Hook can be added.*

13. Cut two 6" (15.2 cm) pieces 26-gauge round dead-soft wire. Coil one 6" (15.2 cm) wire around an EE2 or EE4 Arched Loop five to six times. On a second EE-shape cluster, repeat with the second 6" (15.2 cm) wire. String a daisy spacer, rondelle, and daisy spacer onto one wire, then thread the second wire through the opposite end of the daisy spacer, rondelle, and daisy spacer so the wires cross inside the spacers and bead **(figure 6)**.

14. Pull the wire tails so the spacers and bead are against the clusters, then coil one wire one time around the opposing EE2 or EE4 Arched Loop. Repeat this with the second wire. Work back and forth, coiling each wire a total of five to six times. Working back and forth helps to keep from pulling the wire too tightly. Cut the wire tails.

15. Repeat Steps 13 and 14 until all of the EE-shape clusters are coiled together.

16. Attach two 4mm jump rings to the EE shape on one end of the bracelet, with one jump ring on each side of the EE shape's center loop. Repeat on the other end of the bracelet, then attach the loop of the Elegant Elle Hook to those jump rings.

17. If desired, you can attach the small loop of an Elegant Elle Eye to the first set of 4mm jump rings added in Step 16.

    Note: *To make a chain extender, slide a daisy spacer, rondelle, and daisy spacer onto a head pin and make a Wrapped Loop, but before wrapping the loop closed, slide the loop through the end of the 1" (2.5 cm) chain. Then, wrap the loop closed. Attach the chain to the first set of 4mm jump rings added in Step 16. Alternatively, attach the chain to the 5 mm loop of the Elegant Elle Eye added in Step 17.*

18. Check for any sharp edges and push them down or file them as needed.

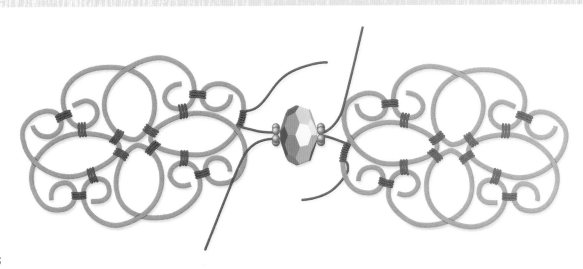

Fig. 6

Judy's Earrings

When I saw these fabulous turquoise briolettes, I had to have them. I was so inspired that designing wire filigree around them was a snap! The oxidized sterling silver wire and beads complement the cool tones of the briolettes, and the double Shepherd's Hooks create an elegant frame. For Aunt Judy, one of my best friends.

Techniques

◊ *Oxidizing Wire (page 30)*
◊ *Shepherd's Hooks (page 25)*
◊ *Coiling (page 28)*
◊ *Adding a Bead (page 28)*
◊ *Jump Rings (optional; page 18)*
◊ *Ear Wires (page 27)*

Finished Measurement

2¾" (7 cm), including ear wire

Project Notes

Because square wire is perfect for twisting and adds a nice aesthetic to any piece of jewelry, I used both 18-gauge round and square dead-soft wire for my wire frames. If you want your earrings longer, add chain instead of jump rings to the tops of the Shepherd's Hooks. I decided to oxidize the sterling silver for this project. When oxidizing small beads, it can be tricky to clean off the excess Silver Black or Liver of Sulfur (LOS), because the beads are so difficult to hold on to. What I found works well is to string the beads on wire, then twist the wire onto itself to keep the beads from coming off. Place the beads against a hard surface, then use steel wool to clean the beads. It's best to oxidize the wire (except the wire used for the ear wires) and jump rings before you make the piece.

MATERIALS

- 32" (81.2 cm) of 18-gauge square dead-soft wire
- 10½" (26.7 cm) of 18-gauge round dead-soft wire
- 4' (1.2 m) of 26-gauge round dead-soft wire
- 4½" (11.4 cm) of 20-gauge round half-hard wire (ear wires)
- 2 turquoise 10.5 × 39mm top-drilled briolettes
- 4 round 2mm beads
- 4 round 3mm beads
- 10 round 20-gauge 4mm jump rings, store-bought or handmade
- 8 round 20-gauge 5mm jump rings, store-bought or handmade

TOOLS

- Flush cutters
- 2/2.5 and 3/5mm bail-making pliers or round-nose pliers
- Chain-nose pliers
- Flat-nose pliers
- Ring mandrel
- Nylon-jaw wire-straightening pliers
- Ruler
- Low-stick tape
- Silver Black or LOS, bowl, and tongs

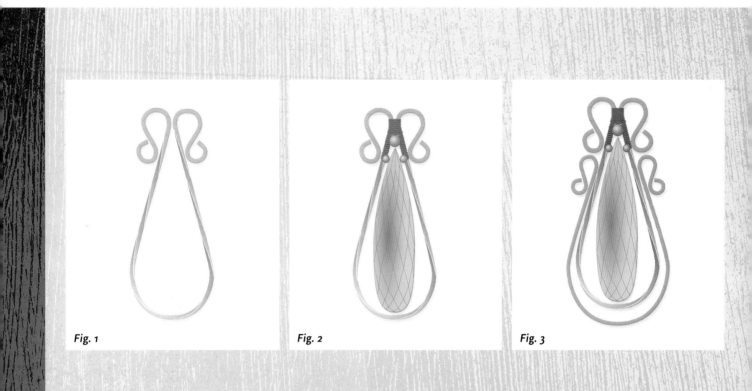

Fig. 1 Fig. 2 Fig. 3

1. **Twisted Wire Frame:** Straighten and flush-cut 6½" (16.5 cm) of 18-gauge square dead-soft wire. With a permanent marker, mark the center of the wire.

2. Make Shepherd's Hooks on both wire ends using 3mm bail-making or round-nose pliers for the small loops and 5mm bail-making or round-nose pliers for the hooks, with the hooks made on the same side of the wire.

3. Holding each Shepherd's Hook between your fingers, twist the wire two full times around until both hooks are again on the same side of the wire.

4. Hold the center mark against size 5 on a ring mandrel and shape the wire around the mandrel until the hooks touch, forming a teardrop shape. Remove the permanent marker mark *(figure 1)*.

5. With 12" (30.5 cm) of 26-gauge round dead-soft wire, coil the Shepherd's Hooks together six to seven times, then add a 3mm round bead. Cut the wire tails.

6. With the remaining 26-gauge round dead-soft wire, coil the Shepherd's Hooks frame, starting under the 3mm round bead, six to seven times.

   Note: *The number of times coiled may vary, depending on the location of the bead hole. String a 2mm bead, the briolette, and a 2mm bead onto the wire, then coil the other side of the*

Shepherd's Hooks frame six to seven times. Cut the wire tails *(figure 2)*.

7. **Round Wire Frame:** Straighten and flush-cut 5¼" (13.3 cm) of 18-gauge round dead-soft wire. With a permanent marker, mark the center of the wire.

8. Make Shepherd's Hooks on both wire ends using 2mm bail-making or round-nose pliers for the small loops and 3mm bail-making or round-nose pliers for the hooks, with the hooks made on the same side of the wire.

9. Hold the center mark against size 13 on a ring mandrel and shape the wire around the mandrel, forming a teardrop shape. When this frame is placed around the twisted wire frame, the top of the Shepherd's Hooks should touch the bottoms of the Shepherd's Hooks of the twisted wire frame *(figure 3)*.

10. **Twisted Bottom Pieces:** Straighten and flush-cut 1½" (3.8 cm) of 18-gauge square dead-soft wire. With a permanent marker, mark the center of the wire. With 2mm bail-making pliers, make a loop on each wire end with the loops on the same side of the wire.

Fig. 4

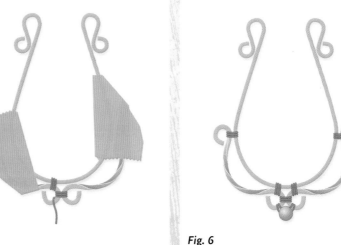

Fig. 5

Fig. 6

11. Holding each loop between your fingers, twist the wire one full time around until the loops are again on the same side of the wire.

Note: It is easier to hold one loop with nylon-jaw wire-straightening pliers and hold the second loop with your dominant hand to twist.

12. Hold the center mark against size 1 on a ring mandrel and shape the wire around the mandrel. Remove the permanent marker mark *(figure 4)*.

13. Repeat Steps 10–12, creating a second twisted bottom piece.

14. Tape the two twisted bottom pieces to the round wire frame, centering the loops at the permanent marker mark on the round wire frame.

15. With 12" (30.5 cm) of 26-gauge round dead-soft wire, coil a loop of the twisted bottom pieces to the round wire frame three to four times, ending the coil by bringing the wire tail up inside the loop. Do not cut the wire tail. With the remaining wire tail, coil the two loops of the twisted bottom pieces together three to four times. Do not cut the wire tail *(figure 5)*.

16. Remove the permanent marker mark. With 4" (10.2 cm) of 26-gauge round dead-soft wire, coil the loop of the second twisted bottom piece to the round wire frame three to four times. Cut the wire tails.

17. With the wire tail from Step 15, add a 3mm bead. Cut the wire tails.

18. Remove the tape from one of the twisted bottom pieces. If needed, cut 12" (30.5 cm) of 26-gauge round dead-soft wire or with the remaining 26-gauge round dead-soft wire from Step 17, coil the top loop of the twisted bottom piece to the round wire frame three to four times. Repeat these actions on the second top loop of the twisted bottom piece *(figure 6)*.

19. With two 4mm jump rings, attach the top of the Shepherd's Hook of the round wire frame to the bottom of the Shepherd's Hook of the twisted wire frame. Repeat this on the second two hooks.

20. Attach two 5mm jump rings to the top left Shepherd's Hook of the twisted wire frame. Repeat this on the top right shepherd's hook.

21. Attach one 4mm jump ring through the four jump rings from Step 20.

22. Straighten and flush-cut 2¼" (5.7 cm) of 20-gauge round half-hard wire. Make an ear wire. Attach the ear wire to the 4mm jump ring from Step 21.

23. Repeat Steps 1–22 for the second earring.

Isabella's Pendant

I found these beautiful cherry quartz briolettes at a bead show. Make the pendant with Swarovski crystals to match Misti's Bracelet (page 52) or mix it up and use semiprecious stones. After making this pendant I thought of my friend's pug, Isabella, who is a total princess. Maybe next time I'll make one for her collar!

Techniques

◊ Regal Scroll (page 24)
◊ Regal Shape (page 25)
◊ Weave Pattern (page 29)
◊ Coiling (page 28)
◊ Adding a Bead (page 28)
◊ Five-Loop Cloverleaf (page 21)
◊ Jump Rings (optional; page 18)
◊ Elegant Elle Hook (page 26)
◊ Elegant Elle Eye (page 27)
◊ Straight Three-Loop
   Cloverleaf (page 20)

Finished Measurements

Pendant: 2½" (6.4 cm); **chain and clasp:** 22" (55.9 cm)

Project Notes

Follow the Regal Scroll instructions in the Essential Techniques chapter with this exception: you'll flush-cut each Regal Scroll at 3" (7.6 cm) and make 2 mm loops. You'll weave two Regal Scrolls together to make each Regal Shape. The cherry quartz briolettes are from Rocky's Designs.

PENDANT MATERIALS

- 14" (35.6 cm) of 18-gauge round dead-soft wire
- 6'–7' (1.8–2.1 m) of 26-gauge round dead-soft wire
- 1 sterling silver 5mm bicone bead
  Note: The bead hole needs to accommodate 26-gauge dead-soft wire passing through twice.
- 1 glass, crystal, or semiprecious 20mm triangular-shaped top-drilled briolette
- 1 glass, crystal, or semiprecious 8mm round teardrop-shaped top-drilled briolette
- 4 round 3mm 20-gauge jump rings

CHAIN MATERIALS

- 4'–5' (1.2–1.5 m) of 18-gauge round dead-soft wire
- 64 round 18-gauge 5mm jump rings, store-bought or handmade

TOOLS

- Nylon-jaw wire-straightening pliers
- Flush cutters
- Chain-nose pliers
- 2/2.5, 3/5 and 7/9mm bail-making pliers or round-nose pliers
- Ring mandrel
- Ruler
- Low-stick tape

Fig. 1

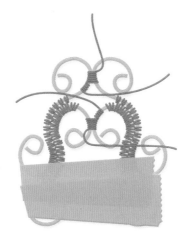
Fig. 2

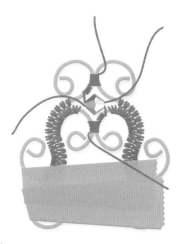
Fig. 3

1. Make two Regal Scrolls using 3" (7.6 cm) of 18-gauge round dead-soft wire each.

2. Tape one end of each Regal Scroll together then follow the Regal Shape instructions, using 18" (45.8 cm) of 26-gauge round dead-soft wire to weave the Regal Scrolls together. Weave from one outside loop to the second outside loop, removing the tape to finish weaving. Cut both wire tails.

3. Repeat Steps 1 and 2, then tape the woven Regal Shapes together as shown. With 9" (22.9 cm) of 26-gauge round

dead-soft wire, coil the top two loops together six to seven times, starting the coil at the top of the two arches and coiling toward the center opening in between the two pieces. Next, coil the curve on the left loop four to five times. Do not cut the wire tails *(figure 1)*.

4. Remove and reposition the tape as needed. With 20" (50.8 cm) of 26-gauge round dead-soft wire and leaving a 9" (22.9 cm) tail, coil the next set of loops together six to seven times, starting the coil next to the small loops and coiling toward the center opening in between the pieces. Next, coil the curve of the arch on the right four to five times. Do not cut the wire tails *(figure 2)*.

   Note: The 9" (22.9 cm) tail will be used in Step 6 to add the center briolette.

5. String the 5mm bicone bead onto the wire tail from Step 4, then thread the wire tail from Step 3 through the opposite end of the bicone bead so the wires cross inside the bead. Pull the wire tails so the bead is centered in between the two pieces *(figure 3)*.

6. With the wire tails, coil the curve of the top right loop and the arch of the bottom left loop four to five times, coiling toward the center coils in Steps 3 and 4. Cut all wire tails except for the 9" tail from Step 4 *(figure 4)*.

7. Remove the tape. With the 9" (22.9 cm) wire tail from Step 4, add a bead, connecting the 20mm triangular

Fig. 4

Fig. 5

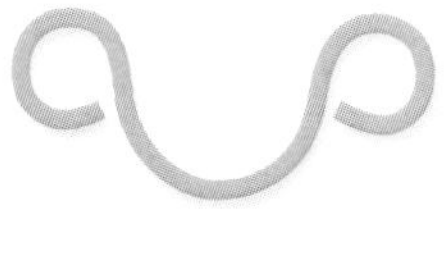

Fig. 6

Fig. 7

briolette. If necessary, before adding the briolette, make a few additional coils connecting the loops so you can wrap between the small loop and down the small loop until there is enough space for the briolette to hang. Finish by coiling the other small loops, coiling up toward the center coil. Cut the wire tails *(figure 5)*.

8. With 18-gauge round dead-soft wire, create a Five-Loop Cloverleaf, making the four outside loops 2 mm and the center loop 3 mm.

9. To attach the 8mm briolette to the Five-Loop Cloverleaf, cut 6" (15.2 cm) of 26-gauge round dead-soft wire and string 2" (5.1 cm) through the briolette. Cross the 2" (5.1 cm) and 4" (10.2 cm) wire ends, forming a triangle.

10. With chain-nose pliers, make a slight bend in the 4" (10.2 cm) wire to straighten it, then coil the 2" (5.1 cm) wire around the 4" (10.2 cm) wire three times. Cut the 2" (5.1 cm) wire tail.

11. With the 4" (10.2 cm) wire tail, make a wrapped loop but before you wrap the loop closed, attach it to the center loop of the Cloverleaf. Cut the wire tail.

12. Attach the two outside loops of the Cloverleaf to the bottom of the woven Regal Shapes, using two 3mm jump rings on each side.

13. Make an Elegant Elle Hook with 3" (7.6 cm) of 18-gauge round dead-soft wire and an Elegant Elle Eye using 2⅝" (6.7 cm) 18-gauge round dead soft wire.

14. *Straight Three-Loop Cloverleaf Chain:* Make 28 Straight Three-Loop Cloverleaf shapes with 18-gauge round dead-soft wire and 3 mm loops.

15. Flush-cut 1½" (3.8 cm) of 18-gauge round dead-soft wire. Mark the center with a permanent marker. Hold the mark against a 7mm mandrel and shape the wire into a U. Remove the permanent marker mark *(figure 6)*.

16. Using 3mm bail-making pliers or round-nose pliers, make loops on each wire end with the loops facing outward from the center of the U. Attach each side of the U-shape with two 5mm jump rings to the arches on top of the pendant *(figure 7)*.

17. Use two 5mm jump rings each to connect fourteen Cloverleaf shapes together, then connect the Elegant Elle Hook to one end of the chain. Connect the opposite end of the chain to a loop on the U-shaped piece.

18. Repeat Step 17 to complete the other side of the chain and connect the Elegant Elle Eye.

Denise's Earrings

These earrings are one of my favorite projects in the book. Bold yet refined, they can be dressed up or down. I prefer to wear them with jeans and a cute tee. Make just one more to create a matching pendant! I named this project for my fellow jewelry designer Denise Peck, who loves earrings; when she saw these, she said she had to have them.

Techniques

◊ *Regal Loop (page 17)*
◊ *Modified Elegant Elle (EE; page 22)*
   Note: *Modified Elegant Elle shape (MEE) described in instructions.*
◊ *Coiling (page 28)*
◊ *Adding a Bead (page 28)*
◊ *Ear Wires (page 27)*
◊ *Jump Rings (optional; page 18)*

Finished Measurement

3¼" (8.3 cm) long, including ear wire

Project Notes

I used 18-gauge round sterling silver dead-soft wire for the modified Elegant Elle (MEE) shapes and 26-gauge round sterling silver dead-soft wire for coiling. To modify the EE shapes, I incorporated Regal Loops for the two outside loops of the EE shape, using 7mm and 2mm bail-making pliers. For the frames, I used 18-gauge square sterling silver dead-soft wire. If I had used all round wire, the pieces would have rolled up on top of each other. You can use all square for the earrings or make the MEE shapes square and the frame round, but I wouldn't use all round wire.

MATERIALS

• 20" (50.8 cm) of 18-gauge square dead-soft wire
• 13" (33 cm) of 18-gauge round dead-soft wire
• 4½" (11.4 cm) of 20-gauge round half-hard wire (ear wires)
• 13'–14' (4–4.3 m) of 26-gauge round dead-soft wire
• 2 4mm bicone beads
   Note: *The bead holes need to accommodate 26-gauge wire passing through twice.*
• 4 round 3mm beads
• 3" (7.6 cm) of commercial chain
• 6 round 3mm 20-gauge jump rings, store-bought or handmade

TOOLS

• Nylon-jaw wire-straightening pliers
• Chain-nose pliers
• Flush cutters
• 2/2.5, 3/5, and 7/9mm bail-making pliers or round-nose pliers
• Flat-nose pliers
• Ruler
• Low-stick tape
• Permanent marker
• Gridded composition paper

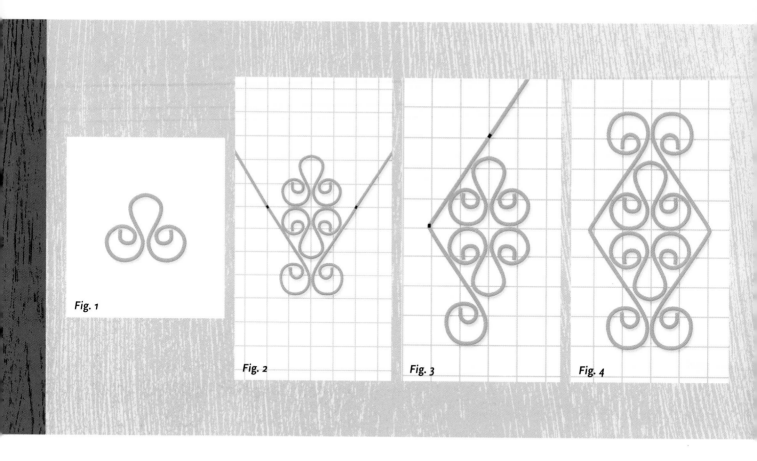

Fig. 1

Fig. 2

Fig. 3

Fig. 4

1. Straighten and flush-cut four 3¼" (8.3 cm) pieces of 18-gauge round dead-soft wire. With a permanent marker, mark the center of each piece.

2. Make two Regal Loops on the 3¼" (8.3 cm) lengths of wire with the loops on the same side of the wire. Repeat this step on the remaining three 3¼" (8.3 cm) pieces of 18-gauge round dead-soft wire.

3. To shape the wire into a U, hold the mark made in Step 1 against a 5mm mandrel (or 5mm bail-making pliers), then push the looped ends evenly around the mandrel until the Regal Loops touch. Remove the mark. Repeat this step on the remaining three pieces of 18-gauge wire **(figure 1)**. These are the four modified MEE pieces.

4. Straighten and flush-cut four 5" (12.7 cm) lengths of 18-gauge square dead-soft wire to create the frames. Make a Regal Loop on one end of each 5" (12.7 cm) piece of 18-gauge square dead-soft wire.

5. Center one pair of MEE shapes on gridded composition paper lines with the Regal Loops touching. Place two of the 5" (12.7 cm) frame wires from Step 4 next to the MEE shapes with the wires touching the three loops of the bottom MEE shape. Mark each 5" (12.7 cm) wire where it aligns with the center of the MEE shape **(figure 2)**.

6. Starting with one frame wire, use flat-nose pliers to make a bend at the mark, creating a V shape. Place the wire next to the MEE shapes. The wire needs to touch the bottom and top loops of the top MEE shape. If the wire does not touch the loops, adjust the bend. Mark the wire at the top where it intersects with the graph line and the center of the MEE shapes **(figure 3)**.

7. Measure 1¼" (3.2 cm) from the mark made in Step 6 and flush-cut the wire. This is the length of wire required to make a 7 mm Regal Loop with 18-gauge square dead-soft wire.

   Note: *To learn how to calculate how much wire is used for loops, please see the instructions for P-Shaped Loops (page 14).*

8. Make a Regal Loop on the end of the wire. The loop should face in the same direction as the loop at the other end of the wire. Remove the permanent marker marks. Repeat Steps 6 and 7 with the second frame wire **(figure 4)**.

9. Repeat Steps 5–8 with the other two 5" (12.7 cm) frame wires and pair of MEE shapes.

10. Cut two 12" (30.5 cm) pieces of 26-gauge round dead-soft wire. Coil the center of an MEE shape together four to five times then coil one Regal Loop two to three times next to where you coiled the center. Do not cut the wire. With the second 12" (30.5 cm) of 26-gauge round dead-soft wire,

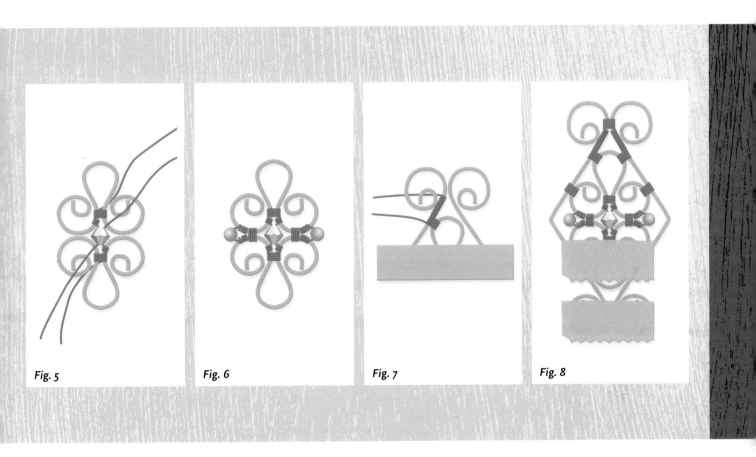

Fig. 5

Fig. 6

Fig. 7

Fig. 8

repeat this on a second MEE shape, finishing by coiling the diagonal Regal Loop.

11. String a 4mm bicone bead onto one wire tail, then thread the second wire tail through the opposite end of the bicone bead so the wires cross inside the bead. Pull the wire tails to center the bicone bead between the two MEE shapes (*figure 5*).

12. Coil the second Regal Loop of each MEE shape two to three times. Cut all wire tails.

13. With the remaining 26-gauge wire, add a bead, coiling the middle of the Regal Loops on one side together five to six times, then coil one Regal Loop five times. String a round 3mm bead, then coil the wire to the other Regal Loop five more times. Cut the wire. Repeat this step on the other two Regal Loops. (*figure 6*).

14. Repeat Steps 10–13 on the second pair of EE shapes.

15. Tape the MEE shapes and frame wires together, leaving the top three loops exposed. With 12" (30.5 cm) of 26-gauge round dead-soft wire, coil the top MEE-shape loop to the frame wire four to five times, then coil the frame wire up to where the frame loops touch. Do not cut the wire tails (*figure 7*).

16. With 12" (30.5 cm) of 26-gauge round dead-soft wire, coil the second side of the top MEE-shape loop to the frame wire four to five times, then coil the frame wire up to where the frame loops touch. Next, coil the two frame wires together four to five times. Cut all wire tails.

17. Remove and reposition tape, exposing the two loops of the MEE. With the remaining wire from Step 16, coil each Regal Loop on this MEE shape to the frame four to five times. Cut the wire tails (*figure 8*).

18. Repeat Step 16 on the second MEE shape. Next, repeat Steps 15 and 16 (no tape is necessary), coiling the center MEE-shape loop to the frames, then coiling the two loops of the frame together. Cut additional 26-gauge round dead-soft wire as needed.

19. Repeat Steps 15–18 on the second set of MEE shapes and wire frames.

20. Using 4½" (11.4 cm) of 20-gauge round half-hard wire, make two ear wires.

21. Cut four ¾" (1.9 cm) pieces of chain. With one 3mm jump ring, attach one chain piece to each top loop of the frame. Repeat this on the second earring.

22. Attach the two pieces of chain to a 3mm jump ring, then attach the jump ring to an ear wire. Repeat this on the second earring.

Charli's Bracelet

Elegant Elle shapes interlock to create a sinuously flowing design. An Elegant Elle Hook and a pretty bead dangle give it sparkle, perfect for my sister Charli's sparkling personality.

Techniques
◊ *Elegant Elle Hook (page 26)*
◊ *Elegant Elle (EE; page 22)*
◊ *Coiling (page 28)*
◊ *Wrapped Loop (page 16)*

Finished Measurement
7⅝" (19.4 cm)

Project Notes
I used 16-gauge square sterling silver dead-soft wire for the shapes and 20-gauge half-round dead-soft wire for coiling. My small loops are 2.5mm. I've found when making this bracelet that sometimes the Elegant Elle shapes are close to identical, but don't fit together exactly. However, they can be adjusted, which is discussed and illustrated in the project instructions.

MATERIALS
- 32" (81.3 cm) of 16-gauge square dead-soft wire
- 5'–6' (1.5–1.8 m) of 20-gauge half-round dead-soft wire
- 2 round 8mm 16-gauge jump rings or size needed for your hook to fit through
- 1" (2.5 cm) of commercial chain
- 1 head pin
- 1 round 13mm bead
- 2 round 4mm daisy spacers

TOOLS
- Nylon-jaw wire-straightening pliers
- Flush cutters
- Flat-nose pliers
- 2/2.5, 3/5 and 7/9mm bail-making pliers or round-nose pliers
- Chain-nose pliers
- Ring mandrel
- Ruler
- Low-stick tape
- Permanent marker
- Nylon-jaw bracelet-forming pliers or bracelet mandrel
- Metal file

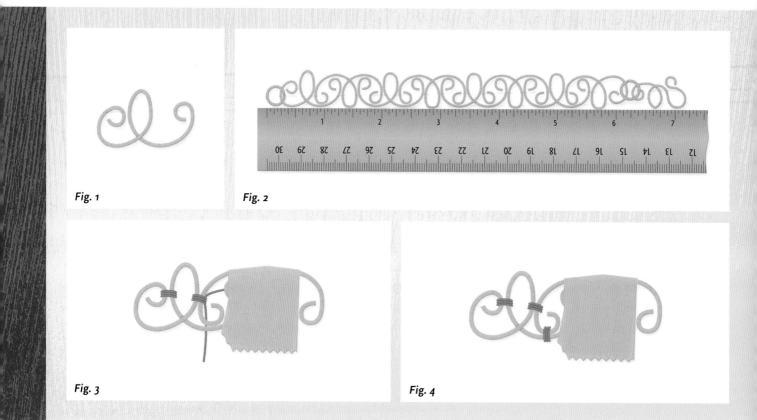

Fig. 1

Fig. 2

Fig. 3

Fig. 4

1. Make an Elegant Elle Hook using 3⅛" (7.9 cm) of 16-gauge square dead-soft wire, except use 2.5mm bail-making pliers to make the small loop described in Step 3 of the Elegant Elle Hook instructions (page 26).

2. Make six Elegant Elle (EE) shapes using 3½" (8.9 cm) of 16-gauge square dead-soft wire for each shape. When you make the small loops, leave them slightly open for ease of coiling the pieces together. Make two additional EE shapes using 3½" (8.9 cm) of 16-gauge square dead-soft wire per shape with one outside loop touching the center loop. These are the end pieces for the bracelet (*figure 1*).

   Note: *Eight EE shapes will yield approximately a 6½" (16.5 cm) long bracelet. Add or subtract EE shapes according to your desired bracelet length, being sure to add in the length of your looped Elegant Elle Hook and two 8mm jump rings. With the addition or subtraction of the shapes being a little over ¾" (1.9 cm), your shapes plus the Elegant Elle Hook and jump rings may not be the exact length needed for your bracelet. You can use a chain extender to achieve your desired length.*

3. Lay the EE shapes out, fitting them together as shown. Laying the shapes out against a ruler ensures that all the pieces are straight or as close to straight as possible. If your shapes aren't perfectly lined up, no worries! Once the bracelet is shaped, your eye won't focus on the alignment (*figure 2*). (See Fitting the Shapes on page 103 for tips.)

Note: *When you assemble the bracelet, it is important to coil the pieces together as they are laid out because they are fitted together. As you coil the pieces together, remember to tighten the coiling wire tails before cutting.*

4. With 12" (30.5 cm) of 20-gauge half-round dead-soft wire, coil the small loop that touches the center loop of both end pieces three times. Cut the wire tails.

   Note: *Coil the same number of times (three) throughout the entire bracelet.*

5. Tape together an end piece and the next EE shape (EE2) that was fitted to the end piece, then coil the center loop of the end piece to the outside body/loop of EE2 three times. Do not cut the wire tails. Turn the wire with your fingers or with the tip of the chain-nose pliers so the flat side of the wire is against the back of the EE shape and the wire coil is in the direction needed for Step 6 (*figure 3*).

6. Coil the curve of the end piece EE to the small loop of EE2. Cut the wire tails (*figure 4*).

7. Remove the tape. Because I coil from left to right, I turn the piece and hold it upside down from Step 6. Coil the center loop of EE2 to the outside body/loop of the end piece EE three times. Do not cut the wire tails (*figure 5*).

8. Reposition the wire as Step 5 describes, then coil the small loop of the end piece EE to the outside curve of EE2 three times. Cut the wire tails (*figure 6*).

Fig. 5

Fig. 6

Fig. 7

Fitting the Shapes

If your EE shapes don't fit together, here are some techniques for adjusting them.

If the two outside loops of two shapes are touching each other, gently pull on the two outside loops of the shape being added. Doing so will make the center loop smaller, thereby creating more space.

If the two outside loops of two shapes are too far apart, shorten the distance between the outside loop and center loop of the shape being added by using either bail-making or round-nose pliers and slowly pulling the loop closer to the center loop. You can also make the center loop larger by gently pushing the two ends inward

Variation

For a daintier bracelet, you can use 18-gauge square antique copper ParaWire (3" wire for each Elegant Elle, 2.5 mm loops) and 21-gauge half round antique copper ParaWire (yep, I'm in love with this color!). Leave off the bead dangle for a simpler look.

Note: Cut an additional 12" (30.5 cm) of 20-gauge half-round dead-soft wire as needed.

9. Tape EE3 to the bracelet, then coil the small loop of EE3 to the outside curve of EE2, still holding the piece in the same orientation as in Step 8 *(figure 7)*.

10. Reposition the wire as Step 5 describes, then coil the outside body/loop of EE3 to the center loop of EE2. Cut the wire tails.

11. Remove the tape and turn the piece, holding it in the same orientation as in Step 6. Coil the outside body/loop of EE2 to the center loop of EE3,

12. Reposition the wire as Step 5 describes, then coil the small loop of EE2 to the outside curve of EE3. Cut the wire tails.

13. Tape EE4 to the bracelet. Coil the center loop of EE3 to the outside body/loop of EE4.

14. Reposition the wire, then coil the small loop of EE4 to the outside curve of EE3.

15. Continue this pattern until all pieces are coiled together.

16. Slide a daisy spacer, bead, and daisy spacer onto a head pin and make a Wrapped Loop, but before wrapping the loop closed, slide the loop through the end of the 1" (2.5 cm) chain. Wrap the loop closed. Attach the chain to one end of the bracelet with an 8mm jump ring.

17. Attach the base loop of the Elegant Elle Hook to the other end of the bracelet with an 8mm jump ring.

18. Shape the bracelet with a nylon-jaw bracelet-forming pliers or around a bracelet mandrel. If necessary, gently bend each EE shape with your fingers to further shape the bracelet. The bracelet will be springy, so once it's shaped, hook the bracelet shut so it retains its shape when not being worn. The coils may shift slightly when you shape the bracelet. Check for any sharp edges and push them down or file them as needed.

Victoria's Pendant

Bold yet feminine, this sophisticated pendant would make the perfect accent for an evening dress. A blue topaz briolette is framed by a trio of Cloverleaf shapes and complemented by blue topaz bicone beads in the dangle.

Techniques

◊ *Adding a Bead (page 28)*
◊ *Coiling (page 28)*
◊ *Straight Three-Loop Cloverleaf (page 21)*
◊ *Scroll (page 23)*
◊ *P-Shaped Loop (page 14)*
◊ *Jump Rings (optional; page 18)*

Finished Measurements

Pendant with dangles: 1¾" (4.4 cm); **chain and clasp:** 21" (53.3 cm)

Project Notes

I used 18-gauge round dead-soft wire for this project. The Cloverleaf-shape loops are 2.5mm. All remaining loops are 2mm. I used a blue topaz briolette with blue topaz (from Rocky's Designs) and Aurora Borealis (AB) opal Swarovski bicones for the dangle. When your pendant is complete, be sure to check for any wire edges that may be sticking up and push them down.

PENDANT MATERIALS

- 18" (45.7 cm) of 18-gauge round dead-soft wire
- 6'–7' (1.8–2.1 m) of 26-gauge round dead-soft wire
- 1 faceted 10mm top-drilled briolette
- 4 round 2mm beads
- 7 crystal 4mm bicone beads
- 4 round 3mm 20-gauge jump rings, store-bought or handmade
- 2 round 7mm 20-gauge jump rings or size needed for your chain to slide through, store-bought or handmade
- Seven 1½" (3.8 cm) or 2" (5.1 cm) head pins

CHAIN AND HOOK MATERIALS

- 22" (55.9 cm) of commercial chain
- Toggle clasp
- 2 round 6mm 16-gauge jump rings, store-bought or handmade

TOOLS

- Nylon-jaw wire-straightening pliers
- Flush cutters
- Flat-nose pliers
- 2/2.5mm bail-making pliers or round-nose pliers
- Chain-nose pliers
- Ring mandrel
- Ruler
- Low-stick tape
- Permanent marker

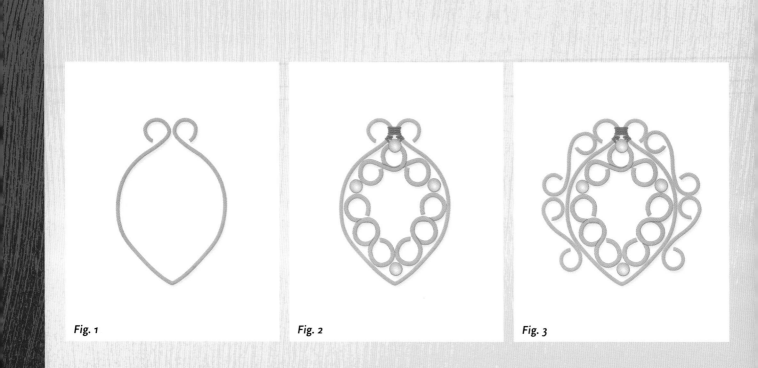

Fig. 1   Fig. 2   Fig. 3

1. **Pendant Frame:** Straighten and flush-cut 3½" (8.9 cm) of 18-gauge round dead-soft wire and mark the center with a permanent marker. With flat-nose pliers, make a bend on the mark, shaping the wire into a wide V.

2. Using 2mm bail-making pliers or round-nose pliers, make a loop on the wire ends that faces outward.

3. Hold the bend against size 13 on a ring mandrel and shape the wire around the mandrel. Push the wire up the mandrel while continuing to gently squeeze the loops together until they touch **(figure 1)**.

   Note: *The frame maintains a rounder shape by starting at a larger size and working up the mandrel.*

4. With 12" (30.5 cm) of 26-gauge round dead-soft wire, add a bead, coiling the two frame loops together three to four times and adding a 2mm round bead. Cut the wire tails.

5. Make three Straight Three-Loop Cloverleaf shapes, but do not push the outside loops completely straight. Leave them slightly curved so they fit against the inside of the frame. Shape the Cloverleaf shapes so that when placed inside the frame, the double-wire center loop is facing the inside of the frame and isn't against the frame. The top Cloverleaf shape will need to be more curved than the two side Cloverleaf shapes. Place the 2mm round beads in between each Cloverleaf shape **(figure 2)**.

6. Straighten and flush-cut four 1" (2.5 cm) pieces of 18-gauge round dead-soft wire. Using 2mm bail-making pliers or round-nose pliers, make four ½" (1.3 cm) long Scrolls and place them on each side of the frame **(figure 3)**.

7. Tape the top two Scrolls to the frame. With 12" (30.5 cm) of 26-gauge round dead-soft wire, coil the top loop of a top Scroll to the corresponding top loop of the frame three to four times. Cut the wire tails. Repeat with the second top loop of a top Scroll/frame loop.

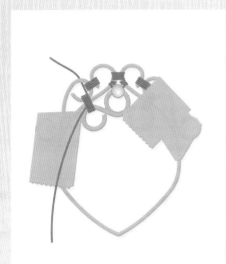

Fig. 4

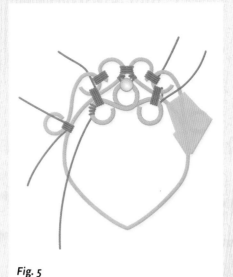

Fig. 5

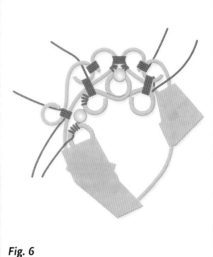

Fig. 6

8. Tape one side of the top Cloverleaf shape inside the frame, then coil the top loop of the top Scroll to the outside loop on one side of the Cloverleaf shape three to four times. Make sure to coil away from yourself, then bring the wire up in between the frame and Scroll loop. Do not cut the wire tails **(figure 4)**.

Note: *If your Scroll and Cloverleaf-shape loops don't line up in Step 9 or upcoming steps, then coil the loops to the frame.*

9. Readjust the tape. Repeat Step 8 on the top loop of the second top Scroll and the second outside loop of the Cloverleaf shape. In this step, you'll need to coil toward yourself so the wire tail ends up properly positioned between the frame and Scroll loop.

Note: *The Cloverleaf shape probably won't stay centered as the Scrolls are being coiled to the pendant. Grab the center loop with the tip of the chain-nose pliers and slide it back to center.*

10. Remove all tape from one side of the frame. With the wire tail from Step 8, coil the outside loop of the Cloverleaf shape three to four times, bringing the wire up on the inside of the frame. With 12" (30.5 cm) of 26-gauge round dead-soft wire, coil the bottom loop of the Scroll to the frame, bringing the wire up inside the Scroll loop **(figure 5)**.

11. String a 2mm round bead onto the Cloverleaf shape wire tail, then position and tape a second Cloverleaf shape to the inside of the pendant. To secure the bead, bring the wire tail behind the outside loop of the second Cloverleaf shape and up through that loop before you coil. Then, coil the wire around the outside loop of the second Cloverleaf shape three to four times. When coiling is complete, bring the wire tail up inside the Cloverleaf-shape loop **(figure 6)**.

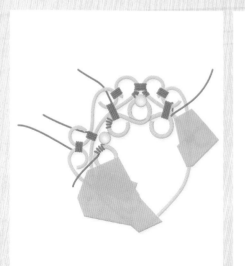

Fig. 7

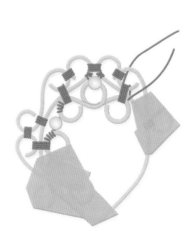

Fig. 8

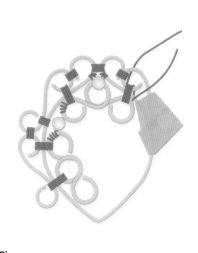

Fig. 9

12. Tape the third Scroll to the outside of the pendant frame. With the Scroll wire tail from Step 10, coil the first and third Scrolls together three to four times *(figure 7)*.

13. With the wire tail from the second Cloverleaf shape, coil the top loop of the third Scroll and the adjacent outside loop of the second Cloverleaf shape three to four times. Tighten and cut all wire tails on the working side of the pendant, leaving the wire tails on the unfinished pendant side *(figure 8)*.

14. Remove the tape. Coil the bottom loop of the third Scroll and the center loop of the second Cloverleaf shape together three to four times. Tighten and cut the wire tails *(figure 9)*.

15. Repeat Steps 10–14 on the other side of the frame with the third Cloverleaf shape and fourth Scroll.

16. Coil both bottom Cloverleaf-shape loops to the pendant frame three to four times *(figure 10)*. Cut the wire tails.

17. With 12" (30.5 cm) of 26-gauge round dead-soft wire, coil the two bottom Cloverleaf loops together three to four times, then add a 2mm round bead *(figure 11)*. Cut the wire tails.

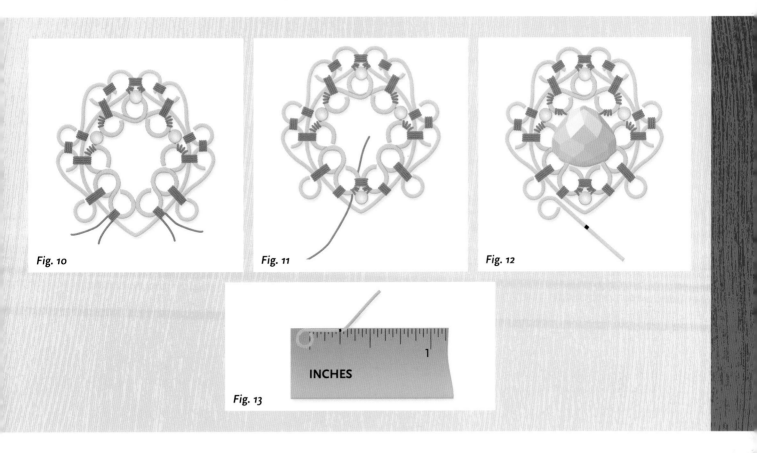

Fig. 10

Fig. 11

Fig. 12

Fig. 13

18. To add the briolette, cut 9" (22.9 cm) of 26-gauge round dead-soft wire. Coil around the left outside loop of the top Cloverleaf (first Cloverleaf added) four to five times coiling toward the center loop, slide the briolette onto the wire, then coil the right outside loop of the top four to five times, coiling toward the frame. Cut the wire tails.

19. Straighten and flush-cut 3" (7.6 cm) of 18-gauge round dead-soft wire. With 2mm bail-making or round-nose pliers, make a P-shaped Loop on one wire end.

Note: Follow the directions for P-Shape Loops to determine how much wire is needed to make this loop, as a duplicate loop is made in Step 21. Place the loop against the bottom loop of the third Scroll. With a permanent marker, mark the point that lines up with the center bottom of the frame **(figure 12)**.

20. With flat-nose pliers, make a slight bend on the mark, forming a wide V. Measure the distance from just inside the loop made in Step 19 to the bend **(figure 13)**.

21. With the measurement from Step 20, add in the amount of wire needed to make another P-shaped loop. Measure from the bend in the wire the total length of these two measurements and flush-cut the wire.

22. Slide an end link of ¼" (6.4 mm) of chain onto the V-shaped wire, then make a P-shaped loop on the second wire end. Place the V shape next to the pendant and, if necessary, adjust the angle of the V to fit next to the frame.

23. Slide a 4mm bicone onto a head pin. Make a wrapped loop but before wrapping the loop closed, attach the loop to a link on the chain. Repeat this six times for a total of seven dangles.

24. Attach the loops of the V shape to the bottom loops of the bottom scrolls using two 3mm jump rings on each side.

25. Attach one 7mm jump ring (or the size needed for your chain to slide through) to each top loop of the frame. Cut 20" (50.8 cm) of chain. Slide the chain through both jump rings. Attach the toggle ring and bar with 6mm jump rings to the ends of the chain.

Jan's Cross

I created this ornate cross for my friend Jan, a kind woman and a dear friend. Graceful Shepherd's Hooks are woven together and accented with twisted and looped L-shapes to showcase a beautiful coiled kyanite stone. You'll get plenty of practice weaving and coiling with this design!

Techniques

◊ *Shepherd's Hook (page 25)*
◊ *Coiling (page 28)*
◊ *Adding a Bead (page 28)*
◊ *Weave Pattern (page 29)*
◊ *Elegant Elle Hook (page 26)*
◊ *Elegant Elle Eye (page 27)*
◊ *Scroll (page 23)*
◊ *Jump Rings (optional; page 18)*

Finished Measurements

Pendant: 2" (5.1 cm); **chain and clasp:** 18½" (47 cm)

Project Notes

It's important to make the Shepherd's Hooks and the twisted L-shapes as symmetrical as possible so the pieces fit together squarely. If you decide to make a sterling silver cross, you may want to practice making the shapes first with copper or craft wire. I used 18-gauge square and 26-gauge round sterling silver dead-soft wire for this project.

CROSS MATERIALS

- 21" (53.3 cm) of 18-gauge square dead-soft wire
- 4" (10.2 cm) of 20-gauge round half-hard or dead-soft craft or copper wire
- 13'–14' (4–4.3 m) of 26-gauge round dead-soft wire
- 1 flat 10mm round focal bead
  Note: *The bead hole needs to accommodate 26-gauge round dead-soft wire passing through three times.*
- 10 round 3mm beads
  Note: *Two of the bead holes need to accommodate 26-gauge round dead-soft wire passing through twice.*

CHAIN AND HOOK MATERIALS

- 3' (91.4 cm) of 18-gauge square dead-soft wire
- 56 round 4mm 20-gauge jump rings, store-bought or handmade

TOOLS

- Nylon-jaw wire-straightening pliers
- Flush cutters
- Chain-nose pliers
- 2/2.5, 3/5 and 7/9mm bail-making pliers or round-nose pliers
- Ruler
- Gridded composition paper
- Low-stick tape
- Permanent marker

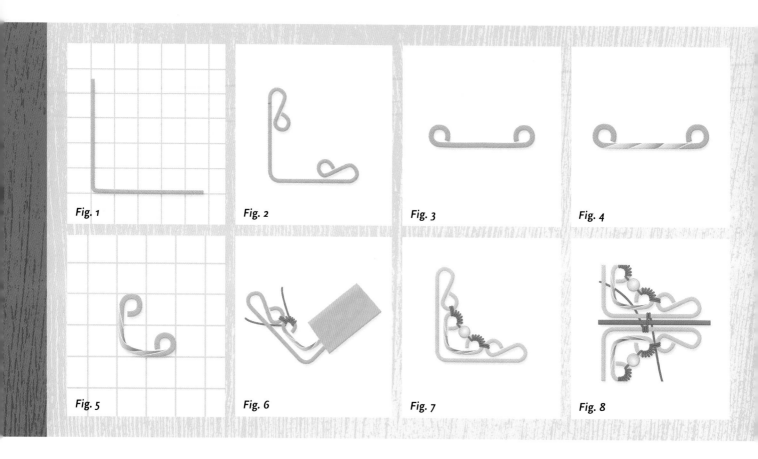

Fig. 1   Fig. 2   Fig. 3   Fig. 4

Fig. 5   Fig. 6   Fig. 7   Fig. 8

1. Straighten and flush-cut four 3¼" (8.3 cm) pieces of 18-gauge square dead-soft wire. With a permanent marker, mark the center of each piece.

2. With flat-nose pliers, bend each wire piece to a 90-degree angle, shaping an L. Place the L-shaped wire on gridded composition paper to make sure that it lines up with the lines on the paper. Repeat this step three times for a total of four L shapes **(figure 1)**.

3. Make Shepherd's Hooks on both ends of each L shape, using 2mm bail-making or round-nose pliers for the small loops and 3mm bail-making or round-nose pliers for the hooks, with the hooks going in toward the center of the L shape **(figure 2)**.

4. When you make the Shepherd's Hooks, the wire will curve, flaring out the wire ends. With flat-nose pliers, squeeze the wire alongside the Shepherd's Hooks to straighten the wire, but leave the curve in the hook. While holding the wire with flat-nose pliers, push the Shepherd's Hooks closed again, because they will open up slightly when you straighten the wire. Check the L shape on gridded composition paper as in Step 2. Remove the permanent marker marks. Repeat Steps 2–4 three times on the remaining pieces of 18-gauge square dead-soft wire.

5. Straighten and flush-cut four 1¼" (3.2 cm) pieces of 18-gauge square dead-soft wire. With a permanent marker, mark the center of each piece. Make 2 mm loops on each wire end, with the loops on the same side of the wire **(figure 3)**.

6. Holding each loop between your fingers, twist the wire one full time around until both loops are again on the same side of the wire.

    Note: *I hold one loop with nylon-jaw wire-straightening pliers and hold the second loop with my dominant hand to twist **(figure 4)**.*

7. Hold the center mark against a 3mm mandrel (3mm jaw of the bail-making pliers) and push the looped ends around the mandrel, creating an L shape. Each L-shaped piece needs to fit in between the Shepherd's Hooks. If a piece does not fit, the loops can be rolled a little more or the bend can be adjusted in or out. Ideally, the shape will line up on gridded composition paper **(figure 5)**.

8. Tape a Shepherd's Hook and twisted L shape together. With 12" (30.5 cm) of 26-gauge round dead-soft wire, coil the Shepherd's Hook loop to the twisted L-shaped loop two to three times. Next, coil the twisted L-shaped loop four to five times **(figure 6)**.

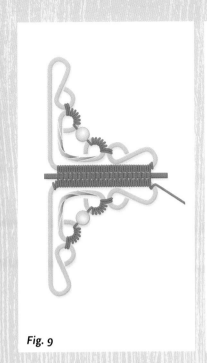

Fig. 9

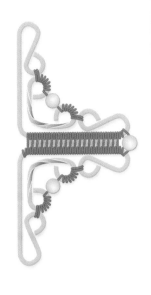

Fig. 10

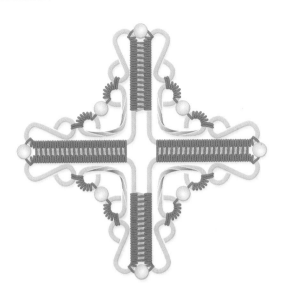

Fig. 11

9. Remove the tape. Slide a 3mm round bead onto the wire, then coil the second twisted L-shaped loop four to five times. Next, coil the twisted L-shaped loop to the Shepherd's Hook loop two to three times. Cut both wire tails *(figure 7)*.

10. Repeat Steps 8 and 9 on the remaining three Shepherd's Hooks and twisted L-shapes. Cut an additional 12" (30.5 cm) of 26-gauge round dead-soft wire as needed.

11. To weave, cut 24" (61 cm) of 26-gauge round dead-soft wire. Coil around one of the Shepherd's Hook pieces two to three times.

    Note: The coil does not have to be started in the corner of the piece. It's a little easier to hang on to the Shepherd's Hook pieces if the coil/weave is started a little way in from the corner. The weave can be pushed toward the corner as more weave is added.

12. To create a space between the shapes when you weave, straighten and cut 3" (7.6 cm) of 18-gauge square dead-soft copper wire and hold this against the coiled Shepherd's Hook piece. Hold a second Shepherd's Hook piece against the wire spacer, then coil one time around the second Shepherd's Hook piece. If desired, tape the pieces together while you weave *(figure 8)*.

13. Follow Steps 3 and 4 of the Weave Pattern instructions in Essential Techniques, weaving to the beginning of the curve on the Shepherd's Hooks. As you weave, push the weave toward the center corners of the Shepherd's Hook pieces. Cut the beginning wire tail, but do not cut the ending wire tail *(figure 9)*.

14. Pull the copper wire spacer out and set aside. Coil three to four times around one Shepherd's Hook, add a 3mm round bead, then coil the second Shepherd's Hook three to four times. Cut the ending wire tail *(figure 10)*.

    Note: Because the cross is made up of four Shepherd's Hooks pieces (four quarters), two quarters are woven together, then the second two quarters are woven together.

15. Repeat Steps 11–14 once, weaving together the two remaining quarter pieces and adding a 3mm round bead. Cut both wire tails.

16. To weave the two halves together and add the 3mm round beads, repeat Steps 11–15 on each half, but don't push the weave to the corners. Instead, the weave needs to start ¼" (6.4 mm) from the corners so there is space to coil the center bead to the cross frame *(figure 11)*.

17. Cut and coil 18" (45.7 cm) of 26-gauge round dead-soft wire around 4" (10.2 cm) of 20-gauge craft or copper wire.

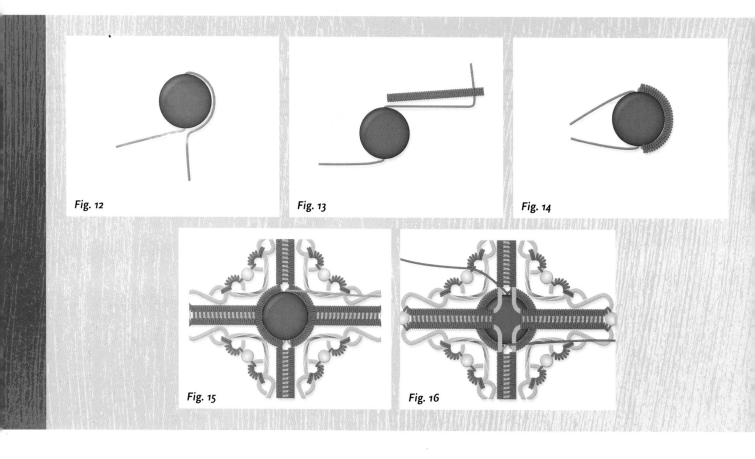

Fig. 12

Fig. 13

Fig. 14

Fig. 15

Fig. 16

18. Remove the coil from the craft wire and cut both wire tails. Cut 10" (25.4 cm) of 26-gauge round dead-soft wire and make a 90-degree bend in the wire at 5" (12.7 cm). Slide the 10mm focal bead onto the wire, with the bead against the 90-degree bend.

19. Pull the wire around the bead and, with your fingers, bend the wire at the point where it meets the bead hole *(figure 12)*.

20. To determine where to cut the coil to fit one-half of the bead, straighten the curve in the wire, taking care not to pull out the bend made in Step 19. Place the coil next to this section of the wire. It is better to cut the coil a little too long than to cut it too short, as it can be cut shorter in upcoming steps if necessary. Size two pieces of coil *(figure 13)*.

21. Straighten the bend made in Step 19, slide the coil on, pull the wire around the bead, then thread the wire end through the bead hole, pulling tightly on both wire ends. If necessary, remove the coil and cut it shorter.
Note: The wire will spring back when released but will be tightened in upcoming steps (figure 14).

22. Slide the second piece of coil onto the second wire end, pull the wire around the bead, then thread the wire end through the bead hole. If necessary, remove the coil and cut it shorter.

23. Check to make sure that there is enough space to coil the wires to the center of the cross. Pull the wire tails snugly then, with your fingers, bend the wire tails at a 90-degree angle to the bead. Place the bead on top of the cross. The weave should end just under the coils. If necessary, remove some weave *(figure 15)*.

24. Turn the cross over and thread the wire through the center opening, then coil each wire tail loosely one time to the cross frame. Check to make sure the bead is centered, then pull each wire tail to tighten the coils *(figure 16)*.

25. Coil each wire tail one more time to the cross frame. Do not cut the wire tails.

26. With 8" (20.3 cm) of 26-gauge round dead-soft wire, thread a 3mm round bead onto the wire. Center the bead on the wire, then bend the wire around it *(figure 17)*.

27. From the front of the cross, slide each wire end from Step 26 in between the coil and center bead *(figure 18)*.

28. Turn the cross over and thread the wire through the center of the cross frame. It's easiest to thread the wire through the center, where the opening is larger, then pull the tails up to the bottom of the weave *(figure 19)*.

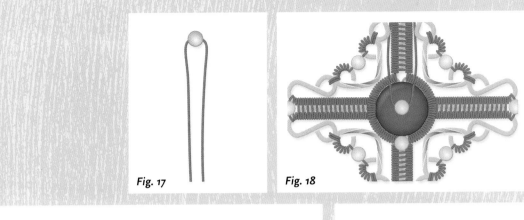

Fig. 17

Fig. 18

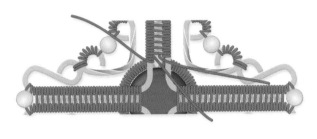

Fig. 19

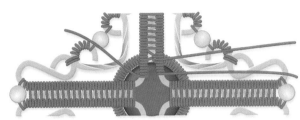

Fig. 20

29. Coil one wire tail around the cross frame, then coil the second wire tail around the same side of the cross frame. The wires will cross over each other when coiling. Coil the two wires to the corner of the cross. Coil the wire tail from Step 25 on the opposite side of the cross frame, coiling to the corner **(figure 20)**.

30. Repeat Steps 26–29 on the other end of the focal bead. Tighten, then cut, all wire tails.

31. Make an Elegant Elle Hook using 3" (7.6 cm) of 18-gauge square dead-soft wire and an Elegant Elle Eye using 2⅝" (6.7 cm) of 18-gauge square dead-soft wire.

32. *Chain:* Make twenty-six Scrolls with 1⅛" (2.9 cm) of 18-gauge square dead-soft wire and 2 mm loops. Twist thirteen Scrolls by holding each loop between your fingers and twisting the wire one full time around until both loops are again on opposite sides of the wire.

33. Connect a total of thirteen Scrolls for one half of the chain, starting with a twisted Scroll connected to a regular Scroll with two 4mm jump rings. Repeat this for the second half of the chain.

34. Attach the Elegant Elle Hook and Elegant Elle Eye with two 4mm jump rings each. Attach each half of the chain to a Shepherd's Hook loop with two 4mm jump rings each.

Jules' Bracelet

My daughter Jules is turning into quite a wonderful young woman, with admirable goals and ambitions. I designed this specially for her, and happily, she loves it as much I loved making it. Make one for someone special in your life!

Techniques
◊ *Elegant Elle Hook (page 26)*
◊ *Elegant Elle Eye (page 27)*
◊ *Regal Loop (page 17)*
◊ *Coiling (page 28)*
◊ *Adding a Bead (page 28)*
◊ *Scroll (page 23)*
◊ *Jump Rings (optional; page 18)*

Finished Measurement
7" (17.8 cm), including clasp

Project Notes
I really love the Regal Loop—it's so versatile! For Jules' Bracelet, you'll make a Regal Loop on one end of the Scrolls. I used 18-gauge square and 26-gauge round sterling silver dead-soft wire. For my beads, I used 3mm and 4mm bicones in between the Scrolls.

MATERIALS
- 5½' (1.7 m) of 18-gauge square dead-soft wire
- 7'–8' (2.1–2.4 m) of 26-gauge round dead-soft wire
- 3 crystal 4mm bicone beads
  Note: The bicone bead holes need to accommodate 26-gauge wire passing through twice.
- 12 crystal 3mm bicone beads
- 20 round 20-gauge 4mm jump rings, store-bought or handmade
- 2 round 16-gauge 7mm jump rings, store-bought or handmade

TOOLS
- Nylon-jaw wire-straightening pliers
- Flush cutters
- Chain-nose pliers
- Flat-nose pliers
- 2/2.5, 3/5 and 7/9mm bail-making pliers or round-nose pliers
- Ruler
- Low-stick tape
- Bracelet mandrel

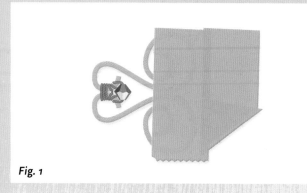

Fig. 1

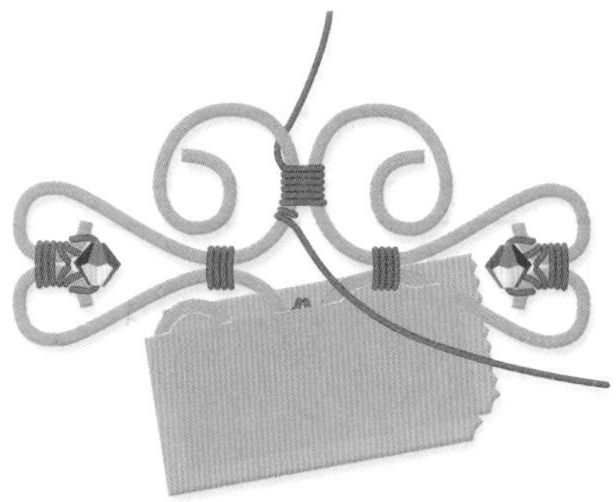

Fig. 2

Fig. 3

Fig. 4

1. Make an Elegant Elle Hook using 3" (7.6 cm) of 18-gauge square dead-soft wire. *Optional:* Make an Elegant Elle Eye using 2⅝" (6.7 cm) of 18-gauge square dead-soft wire.

2. Straighten and flush-cut eight 2" (5.1 cm) pieces of 18-gauge square dead-soft wire.

3. Make a Regal Loop on one end only of each 2" (5.1 cm) piece of wire using 7mm and 2.5mm bail-making or round-nose pliers.

4. On the second end of each 2" (5.1 cm) piece of wire, make a 2.5 mm loop, forming a Scroll.

5. *Centerpiece:* Tape the Regal Loop ends together with the Regal Loops facing outward. The two small loops from Step 4 will be facing toward each other. With 12" (30.5 cm) 26-gauge round dead-soft wire coil the small loops together three to four times, add a 3mm bead *(figure 1)*.

6. Remove the tape and coil the Regal Loops together where the loops touch three to four times.

7. Repeat Steps 5 and 6 on two additional Scrolls.

8. Tape the two sets of Scrolls together, taping the Regal Loop ends back to back. With 12" (30.5 cm) of 26-gauge round dead-soft wire coil two Regal Loops together five to six times, then coil the arch of a Regal Loop one time. Do not cut the wire tails *(figure 2)*.

9. Remove the tape. With 12" (30.5 cm) of 26-gauge dead-soft wire, coil the second two Regal Loops together five to six times, then coil the arch of a Regal Loop one time. Do not cut the wire tails.

10. String a 4mm bead onto one wire tail, then thread the second wire tail through the opposite end of the bead so the wires cross inside the bead. Pull the wire tails so the bead is centered in between the two sets of Scrolls.

11. Coil one wire tail one time around the opposing Regal Loop arch, coiling toward the coil from Step 8. Repeat this with the second wire tail, then coil the second wire tail one more time. Coil the first wire tail a second time. Working back and forth assists in not pulling the wire too tightly and displacing the bead. Cut the four wire tails *(figure 3)*.

12. *Top and Bottom Scrolls:* Place two of the four remaining Scrolls on the top of the centerpiece with the 2.5 mm looped ends toward the center and facing outward. These loops need to touch, so the Regal Loops need to be adjusted smaller. To do so, stick round-nose pliers into the small loop of the Regal Loop and gently pull the loop downward, making the large loop of the Regal Loop smaller. Repeat this on the second Scroll. If necessary, make each Regal Loop of the centerpiece smaller until the outside pieces fit *(figure 4)*.

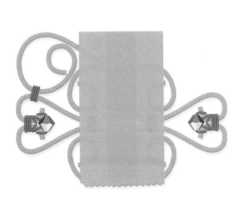

Fig. 5

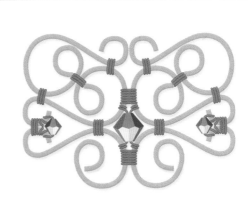

Fig. 6

13. Repeat Step 12, placing the remaining two Scrolls on the bottom of the centerpiece.

14. Tape one top Scroll to the centerpiece. With a piece of remaining 26-gauge round dead-soft wire from Step 11, coil the top Regal Loop to the 2.5 mm loop on the centerpiece three to four times. Cut the wire tails *(figure 5)*.

15. Remove the tape, then coil the top Regal Loop to the centerpiece Regal Loop three to four times. Cut the wire tails.

16. Cut additional 12" (30.5 cm) pieces of 26-gauge round dead-soft wire as needed for coiling. Coil the 2.5 mm loop on the top Scroll to the centerpiece Regal Loop three to four times. Cut the wire tails.

17. Repeat Steps 14–16 on the second top Scroll, coiling it to the centerpiece *(figure 6)*.

18. With 12" (30.5 cm) of 26-gauge round dead-soft wire, coil the 2.5 mm loops on the top Scrolls together, then add a 3mm bicone bead. Cut the wire tails.

19. Repeat Steps 14–18 with the bottom Scrolls from Step 13, coiling them to the centerpiece.

20. *Sidepieces:* Straighten and flush-cut two 1⅛" (2.9 cm) pieces of 18-gauge square dead-soft wire. With a permanent marker, mark the center of each piece.

Fig. 7

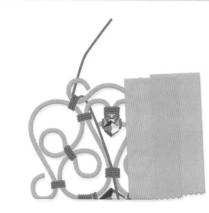

Fig. 8

Fig. 9

21. Working with one 1⅛" (2.9 cm) piece of wire, make a 2 mm sized loop on each wire end, with the loops on the same side of the wire. Hold the center mark against a 9mm mandrel (9mm jaw of the bail-making pliers) and shape the wire around the mandrel. Remove the mark *(figure 7)*.

22. Tape the sidepiece to one side of the centerpiece, leaving one loop exposed. With 26-gauge round dead-soft wire, coil the 2 mm loop to the arch of the Regal Loop three to four times. Bring the wire tail up inside the 2.5mm Scroll loop of the centerpiece *(figure 8)*.

23. Coil the sidepiece loop to the 2.5 mm Scroll loop of the centerpiece three to four times. Cut the wire tails.

24. Remove the tape. With 26-gauge round dead-soft wire, coil the second loop on the sidepiece to the second 2.5 mm Scroll loop on the centerpiece three to four times. Then, coil the sidepiece loop to the arch of the Regal Loop three to four times. Cut the wire tails.

25. Repeat Steps 21–24, coiling the second sidepiece to the other side of the centerpiece.

26. Repeat Steps 2–25 two more times, creating a total of three filigree pieces.

27. *Chain:* Straighten and flush-cut four 2" (5.1 cm) pieces of 18-gauge square dead-soft wire, then repeat Steps 3 and 4.

28. Tape two Scrolls together, with the Regal Loop ends touching and the 2.5 mm looped ends facing outward, leaving one 2.5 mm looped end and Regal Loop arch exposed for coiling.

29. With 26-gauge round dead-soft wire, coil the exposed 2.5 mm looped end to the Regal Loop arch three to four times. Cut the wire tails. Remove the tape, then coil the two Regal Loops together three to four times. Cut the wire tails. Next, coil the second 2.5 mm looped end and Regal Loop arch together three to four times. Cut the wire tails. This comprises one chain link *(figure 9)*.

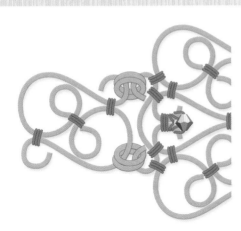

Fig. 10

30. Repeat Steps 27–29, creating a second chain link.

31. Shape the filigree pieces made in Steps 1–25 and the chain pieces on a ring mandrel, giving the pieces a slight curve. To shape the filigree pieces, hold the center of the piece against the ring mandrel at size 15, then shape the sides around the mandrel.

32. Attach the filigree pieces together with four 4mm jump rings, using two jump rings per sidepiece loop.

33. Attach a chain link with two 4mm jump rings, attaching the 2.5 mm loop of the chain link and the Regal Loop of the chain link to sidepiece loops, using two jump rings per sidepiece loop *(figure 10)*.

34. Repeat Step 33, attaching the second chain link to the other end of the bracelet.

35. With two 4mm jump rings, attach the base loop of the Elegant Elle Hook to the 2.5 mm loop of the chain link on one end of the bracelet. Then, attach the base loop of the Elegant Elle Hook to the arch of the Regal Loop of the chain link with two 4mm jump rings.

36. If you did not make an Elegant Elle Eye for the Elegant Elle Hook, attach one 7mm jump ring to the 2.5 mm loop of the chain link and one 7mm jump ring to the arch of the Regal Loop of the chain link.

Variation

To make your bracelet longer or shorter, add or subtract segments of chain, make a Elegant Elle Eye to go with the Elegant Elle Hook, or use a chain extender (see Step 15 of Charli's Bracelet, page 103).

Michelle's Necklace

Filigree doesn't have to be formal! An adorable owl bead is perfectly at home in a setting of Regal Loops. My dear friend Michelle Davis of Tangible Light Studio makes owl and penguin beads, and when I first saw them, I knew I had to have one.

Techniques
◊ *Regal Loop (page 17)*
◊ *Coiling (page 28)*
◊ *Wire Weaving (page 29)*
◊ *Elegant Elle Hook (page 26)*
◊ *Elegant Elle Eye (page 27)*
◊ *Scroll (page 23)*
◊ *Jump Rings (optional; page 18)*

Finished Measurements
Pendant: 1⅜" (3.5 cm); **chain and clasp:** 21" (53.3 cm)

Project Notes
For this project, I used 18- and 26-gauge round sterling silver dead-soft wire. I made my Regal Loops with 5mm and 2mm bail-making pliers and incorporated wire weaving in this design.

PENDANT MATERIAL
- 13" (33 cm) of 18-gauge round dead-soft wire
- 5' (1.5 m) of 26-gauge round dead-soft wire
- 1 lampwork 18mm lentil bead
- 2 crystal 3mm bicone beads

CHAIN MATERIALS
- 6' (1.8 m) of 18-gauge round dead-soft wire
- 60 round 5mm 18-gauge jump rings, store-bought or handmade

TOOLS
- Nylon-jaw wire-straightening pliers
- Flush cutters
- Chain-nose pliers
- 2/2.5, 3/5 and 7/9mm bail-making pliers or round-nose pliers
- Ring mandrel
- Ruler
- Permanent marker
- Low-stick tape

Fig. 1   Fig. 2   Fig. 3

1. *Inner Circle:* Straighten and flush-cut 4¾" (12.1 cm) of 18-gauge round dead-soft wire. Mark the center with a permanent marker.

2. Make a Regal Loop on each end with 5mm and 2mm bail-making or round-nose pliers, with the loops on the same side of the wire.

3. Hold the center mark against size 13 on a ring mandrel and shape the wire into a circle. Because the wire will spring back and the Regal Loops need to touch, slide the wire up to size 12. The Regal Loops may overlap when you push them toward each other. If necessary, repeat this on smaller sizes until, with spring-back, the Regal Loops remain touching. Remove them from the mandrel and remove the center mark *(figure 1)*.

4. *Middle Circle:* Straighten and flush-cut 4¹¹⁄₁₆" (11.9 cm) of 18-gauge round dead-soft wire. Mark the center with a permanent marker. Repeat Step 2.

5. Hold the center mark against size 14 on a ring mandrel and shape the wire around the mandrel. The Regal Loops should not touch each other; rather, when placed around the inner circle, the middle circle Regal Loops should touch the inner circle Regal Loops. If they don't touch, slide the wire up to size 13, or smaller sizes, and push the Regal Loops together until they touch the inner circle Regal Loops. Remove the center mark *(figure 2)*.

6. *Outer Circle:* Straighten and flush-cut 4½" (11.4 cm) of 18-gauge round dead-soft wire. Mark the center with a permanent marker. Repeat Step 2.

7. Hold the center mark against size 15 on a ring mandrel and shape the wire around the mandrel. Repeat Step 5 until the outer circle Regal Loops touch the middle circle Regal Loops when the outer circle is placed around the middle circle. If the outer circle needs to be wider, hold onto each loop and gently pull out. Remove the center mark.

8. *Inner Circle:* Cut 30" (76.2 cm) of 26-gauge round dead-soft wire, then coil the inner circle Regal Loops together eight to ten times.

9. Coil the inner circle on the left side up to the point where the middle circle Regal Loop touches the inner circle *(figure 3)*.

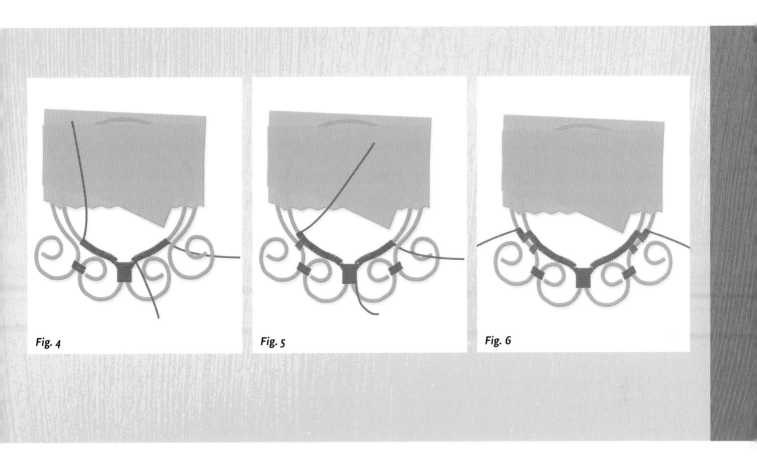

Fig. 4

Fig. 5

Fig. 6

10. Cut 30" (76.2 cm) of 26-gauge round dead-soft wire, then coil the inner circle on the right side starting from the top of the coiled Regal Loops from Step 8, coiling up to the point where the middle circle Regal Loop touches the inner circle.

11. Tape the inner and middle circles together. Tighten and cut the beginning wire tail from Step 8. Cut 12" (30.5 cm) of 26-gauge round dead-soft wire, then coil one inner and one outer Regal Loop together three to four times. Cut the wire tails *(figure 4)*.

12. With the remaining 26-gauge round dead-soft wire from Step 11, coil the other set of inner and outer Regal Loops together three to four times. Cut the wire tails.

13. With the wire tail from Step 9, coil around the inner and middle circles three times, then coil around the inner circle three times *(figure 5)*.

14. Repeat Step 13 with the wire tail from Step 10, coiling around the other side of the middle and inner circles. Cut the beginning wire tail from Step 10.

15. With the wire tail from Step 9, coil around the inner and middle circles three times, then coil around the middle circle three times. Repeat this with the second wire tail from Step 10 *(figure 6)*.

16. Remove the tape, then tape the outer circle to the middle circle. With the remaining 26-gauge round dead-soft wire from Step 11, coil the outer Regal Loops to the next Regal Loop three to four times. Cut the wire tails, then coil the other outer Regal Loop to the next Regal Loop three to four times and cut the wire tails.

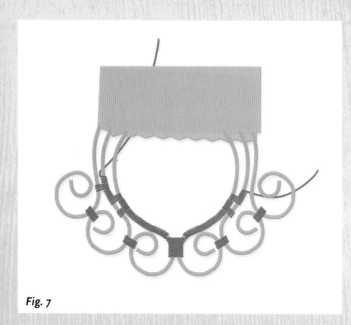

Fig. 7

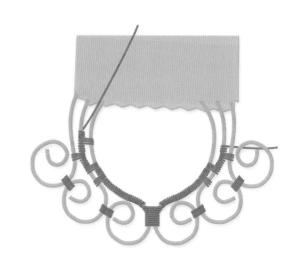

Fig. 8

17. With the wire tail from Step 13, coil around the middle and outer circles three times, then coil around the middle circle three times *(figure 7)*.

18. Repeat Step 17 with the wire tail from Step 14 on the other side of the pendant.

19. With the wire tail from Step 17, coil around the inner and middle circles three times, then coil around the middle circle three times *(figure 8)*.

20. Repeat Step 19 with the wire tail from Step 18 on the other side of the pendant. Reposition or remove the tape as needed.

21. Repeat Steps 17–20, weaving to the top of the circles and leaving the space as shown. After the last three coils around either the inner and middle or middle and outer circles are completed, coil three times around the inner circle with both wire tails. Do not cut the wire tails *(figure 9)*.

22. Thread a 3mm bicone, lentil bead, and a second 3mm bicone bead onto a head pin. Make a wrapped loop, but before you wrap the loop closed, slide the loop through the center of the inner circle in between the coils from Step 21. If necessary, separate the coils on the inner circle (the wire tails were not cut in order to easily locate the end of each coil). Wrap the loop closed, then cut the head pin tail and both wire tails.

23. Make an Elegant Elle Hook using 3" (7.6 cm) of 18-gauge round dead-soft wire and an Elegant Hook Eye using 2⅝" (6.7 cm) of 18-gauge round dead-soft wire.

24. Straighten and flush-cut twenty-eight 2¼" (5.7 cm) pieces of 18-gauge round dead-soft wire. Make Regal Loops on each wire end with 5mm and 2mm bail-making or round-nose pliers, with the loops on opposite sides of the wire, forming a Scroll *(figure 10)*.

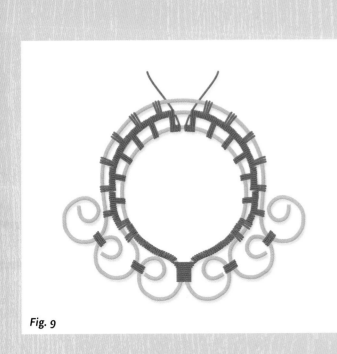

Fig. 9

Fig. 10

25. Assemble the chain with a Scroll, two 5mm jump rings, and another Scroll, connecting a total of fourteen Scrolls for one half of the chain. Attach the base loop of the Elegant Elle Hook to one end of the chain with two 5mm jump rings. Repeat this step to assemble the second half of the chain, attaching the base loop of the Elegant Elle Eye with two 5mm jump rings.

26. Attach one half of the chain to the center of the outside circle with two 5mm jump rings. Repeat this for the second half of the chain.

27. To shape the pendant, hold the pendant with both hands and gently bend the Regal Loops on the bottom of the pendant toward the back.

Franchezka's Necklace

I know my friend Fran loves emerald green, so when I saw this stunning green topaz briolette, I thought of her. Scrolls of straight and twisted antiqued sterling silver wire form a striking setting worthy of this gorgeous gem, and of Fran.

Techniques

◊ *Oxidizing Wire (page 30)*
◊ *Elegant Elle Hook (page 26)*
◊ *Elegant Elle Eye (page 27)*
◊ *Elegant Elle (page 22)*
  Note: *Modified Elegant Elle (MEE) described in instructions.*
◊ *Coiling (page 28)*
◊ *Scroll (page 23)*
◊ *Adding a Bead (page 28)*
◊ *Jump Rings (optional; page 18)*

Finished Measurements

Centerpiece alone: 3" × 3" (7.6 × 7.6 cm); **including length with chain and clasp:** 15½" (39.3 cm)

Project Notes

I used 20-gauge square sterling silver dead-soft wire to make the modified Elegant Elle shape and the Scrolls. I really love being able to twist square wire, because I think it adds nice dimension and a look of elegance to the finished piece.

Note: *As stated in the Scrolls section of the Essential Techniques section, if your Scroll ends up being too long, the loops can be adjusted by rolling them a bit more. If the Scroll is too short, slightly open up the loops. It's best to oxidize the wire and jump rings before you make the piece.*

FILIGREE MATERIALS

- 16¼" (41.3 cm) of 20-gauge square dead-soft wire
- 6'–7' (1.8–2.1 m) of 26-gauge round dead-soft wire
- 1 faceted 16mm top-drilled briolette
- 5 round 2mm beads
- 1 round 3mm bead

CHAIN AND HOOK MATERIALS

- 6" (15.2 cm) of 18-gauge square dead-soft wire
- 28" (71.1 cm) of 20-gauge square dead-soft wire
- 18 round 20-gauge 4mm jump rings, store-bought or handmade

TOOLS

- Nylon-jaw wire-straightening pliers
- Flush cutters
- 2/2.5, 3/5 and 7/9mm bail-making pliers or round-nose pliers
- Chain-nose pliers
- Flat-nose pliers
- Ruler
- Low-stick tape
- Silver Black or LOS, bowl, and tongs
- 0000 steel wool

Fig. 1

Fig. 2

Fig. 3

1. Make an Elegant Elle Hook with 3" (7.6 cm) of 18-gauge square dead-soft wire and an Elegant Elle Eye with 2⅝" (6.7 cm) of 18-gauge square dead-soft wire.

2. **Modified Elegant Elle (MEE) shape:** Straighten and flush-cut 3" (7.6 cm) of 20-gauge square dead-soft wire. With a permanent marker, mark the center of the wire.

3. With 7mm bail-making or round-nose pliers, make a loop on each wire end with the loops on the same side of the wire. Next, follow Step 2 only of the Regal Loop instructions (page 17), using 2mm bail-making or round-nose pliers.

4. Hold the mark against a 5mm mandrel (5mm jaw of the bail-making pliers) and shape the wire around the mandrel, until the Regal Loops are touching. Remove the mark.

5. With 12" (30.5 cm) of 26-gauge round dead-soft wire, coil the MEE shape together where it touches in the center four to five times **(figure 1)**.

6. **Bottom Scrolls:** Straighten and flush-cut two 1⅝" (4.1 cm) pieces of 20-gauge square dead-soft wire. With 5mm bail-making or round-nose pliers, make a loop on each wire end with the loops on opposite sides of the wire. Next, follow Step 2 only of the Regal Loop instructions, using 2mm bail-making or round-nose pliers.

7. Holding each Scroll loop between your fingers, twist the wire one full time around until both loops are again on the opposite side of the wire.

8. Tape the Scrolls to the MEE shape, with the Scroll loops both facing toward the MEE shape and touching the bottom of the MEE-shape loops. With the remaining 26-gauge round dead-soft wire, coil a Scroll loop to the body of the MEE, then coil the Scroll loop to the MEE-shape loop, coiling both three to four times. Cut the wire tails. Repeat the coiling on the second Scroll **(figure 2)**.

9. Remove the tape. With 12" (30.5 cm) of 26-gauge round dead-soft wire, coil the body of a scroll to the center loop of the MEE shape. Where they touch four to five times, add a 2mm bead. Cut the wire tails **(figure 3)**.

10. **Side Scrolls:** Straighten and flush-cut two 1¾" (4.4 cm) pieces of 20-gauge square dead-soft wire. With 5mm bail-making or round-nose pliers, make a loop on each wire end with the loops on opposite sides of the wire. Next, follow Step 2 only of Regal Loop, using 2mm bail-making or round-nose pliers.

    Note: *These Scrolls will be coiled to the MEE-shape loops and twisted Scroll loops in an upcoming step. Set aside.*

11. **Top Scrolls:** Straighten and flush-cut two 2" (5.1 cm) pieces of 20-gauge square dead-soft wire. With 5mm bail-making or round-nose pliers, make a loop on each wire end with

Fig. 4

the loops on opposites sides of the wire. Next, follow Step 2 only of the Regal Loop instructions, using 2mm bail-making or round-nose pliers.

12. *Twisted Wire Pieces:* Straighten and flush-cut two 1¼" (3.2 cm) pieces of 20-gauge square dead-soft wire. Mark the center of each wire piece with a permanent marker. With 2mm bail-making or round-nose pliers, make a loop on each wire end with the loops on the same side of the wire. Holding each loop between your fingers, twist the wire one full time around until both loops are again on the same side of the wire. Twist the second 1¼" (3.2 cm) wire.

    Note: *It's easier to hold one loop with nylon-jaw wire-straightening pliers and hold the second loop with your dominant hand to twist.*

13. Hold the mark against a 9mm mandrel (9mm jaw of the bail-making pliers) and shape around the mandrel. Remove the mark. Repeat this on the second 1¼" (3.2 cm) piece of wire.

14. Next, tape a twisted wire piece to a Scroll from Step 11, with the Scroll and twisted wire piece loops touching. With 26-gauge of round dead-soft wire, coil the two loops together three to four times. Cut the wire tails. Coil the twisted wire loop to the body of the Scroll three to four times. Cut the wire tails *(figure 4)*.

Fig. 5

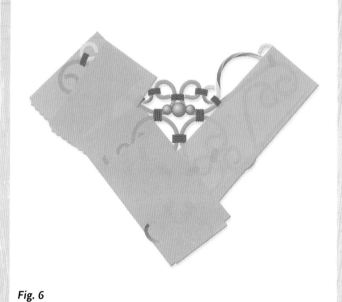

Fig. 6

15. Remove the tape, then with 26-gauge round dead-soft wire, coil the second twisted wire loop to the body of the Scroll. Cut the wire tails.

16. Repeat Steps 14 and 15 on the second Scroll and twisted wire piece.

17. Lay out the pieces on a flat hard surface as illustrated *(figure 5)*.

18. Tape the filigree pieces together, leaving the loops of the top Scrolls exposed.

Note: The side Scrolls need to be taped in place to get an idea of the angle of the top Scrolls, which is based upon the side Scrolls. The angle can be adjusted, if necessary, when the side Scrolls are coiled to the MEE shape in an upcoming step.

19. With 26-gauge round dead-soft wire, coil the top Scroll loops together three to four times. Cut the wire tails.

20. With 26-gauge round dead-soft wire, coil the body of a top Scroll to the arch of the MEE shape three to four times, coiling toward the center of the piece. String a 2mm, 3mm, and 2mm round bead onto the wire, then coil the second body of the top Scroll to the arch of the MEE shape three to four times. Cut the wire tails *(figure 6)*.

21. Reposition the tape on one side of the filigree piece, exposing the side Scroll's bottom loop. With 26-gauge round dead-soft wire, coil the side Scroll bottom loop to the MEE-shape loop three to four times. Bring the wire up inside the side Scroll loop, then coil the side Scroll to the body of the bottom Scroll three to four times. Cut the wire tails.

22. Remove the remainder of the tape on the same side, leaving the second side of the filigree piece taped. If necessary, adjust the angle of the top Scroll/twisted wire piece so it touches the side scroll loop. Coil the side Scroll loop to the body of the top Scroll three to four times. Cut the wire tails.

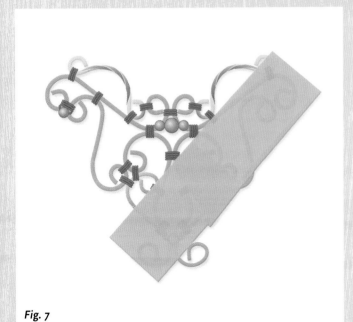

Fig. 7

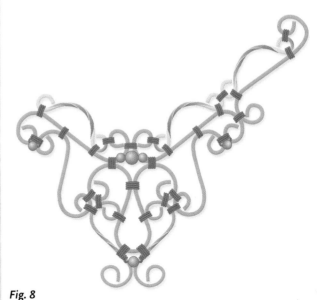

Fig. 8

23. Coil the side Scroll loop to the top Scroll loop three to four times, then add a 2mm bead. Cut the wire tails *(figure 7)*.

24. Repeat Steps 21–23 on the second side of the filigree piece.

25. Repeat Steps 11–16, making two additional Scrolls/twisted-wire pieces. These will be coiled to the existing two Scrolls/twisted wire pieces.

26. Tape a Scroll/twisted wire piece to one already coiled to the filigree piece. With 26-gauge round dead-soft wire, coil the two Scrolls loops together three to four times. Cut the wire tails. Next, coil the two twisted-wire piece loops together three to four times. Cut the wire tails *(figure 8)*.

27. Repeat Step 26 on the second Scroll/twisted-wire piece.

28. *Briolette:* With 26-gauge round dead-soft wire, coil the bottom Scrolls together three to four times, with the coil starting under the 2mm round bead. Next, add the briolette. Cut the wire tails.

29. *Chain:* Straighten and flush-cut sixteen 1¾" (4.4 cm) pieces of 20-gauge square dead-soft wire. With 5mm bail-making or round-nose pliers, make a loop on each wire end with the loops on opposite sides of the wire. Next, follow Step 2 only of the Regal Loop instructions, using 2mm bail-making or round-nose pliers. Twist eight Scrolls by holding each loop between your fingers and twisting the wire one full time around until both loops are on opposite sides of the wire.

30. Connect a total of eight Scrolls for one half of the chain, starting with a twisted Scroll connected to a straight Scroll with one 3mm jump ring. Repeat this step for the second half of the chain.

31. Attach the Elegant Elle Hook and Elegant Elle Eye to an ending Scroll on each chain half with one 3mm jump ring each. Attach each half of the chain to a Scroll with one 3mm jump ring each.

Acknowledgments

Thank you to my Interweave editors—Michelle Bredeson, Allison Korleski, Jane Dickerson, and Erica Smith. I don't know how many ideas I bounced off of you! To Bonnie Brooks, thank you for doing such a fantastic job illustrating the steps in the book. Many thanks to Joe Coca for taking the most amazing photos of the jewelry—wow!

Very special thanks to Bill Coates and Frank Amato, the guys at ParaWire, for everything you have done for me and for making the best craft wire ever!

I thank my kids for their support as I undertook writing my second book. Joanna, I miss you terribly and wish you were here. Jules, thanks for hanging out with me at bead shows in the summer months when school is out, eating your way through the day, and taking naps under the booth table! Joey, thanks for understanding that this is something that I love to do, even though it means we spend time apart. Nick and Zack, love you guys.

Phil, thanks for believing that what I do is "waaaay cool" and for being so proud of me. Your support makes me feel like I can accomplish anything. I love you.

Resources

Check your local bead store for the supplies used in this book, or contact the manufacturers listed below to find out where their products are sold.

WIRE

ParaWire
2-8 Central Ave.
East Orange, NJ 07018
(973) 672-0500
parawire.com

Starr Gems
220 W. Drachman St.
Tucson, AZ 85705
(520) 882-8750
silversupplies.com

Whim-Z Wire by Garlan Chain
Wired Up Beads
726 Commerce St., Ste. 101
Southlake, TX 76092
(817) 421-3030
wiredupbeads.com

FINDINGS AND CHAIN

TierraCast
Check your local bead store or favorite online store.

Primitive Earth Beads
5217 8th Ave. S
Gulfport, FL 33707
(800) 777-0038
primitiveearthbeads.com

SilverSilk & More
P.O. Box 345
Palmerton, PA 18071
(610) 509-5881
silversilkonline.com

STERLING SILVER BEADS

SII Findings
2626 W. Baseline Rd.
Mesa, AZ 85202
(480) 839-0703
siifindings.com

SEMIPRECIOUS STONE BEADS

Bead Palace
163 S. Madison Ave.
Greenwood, IN 46142
(317) 882-9392
beadpalaceInc.com

Rocky's Designs
240-17 68th Ave.
Douglaston, NY 11362
(718) 423-4573

TAJ Company
42 West 48th St.
New York, NY 10036
(212) 944-6330
tajcompany.com

ARTISAN BEADS

Clay River Designs
4375 Hwy 52
Roggen, CO 80652
(303) 849-5234
clayriverdesigns.com

O'Gosh Buttons & Beads
2411 Doty St.
Oshkosh, WI 54902
ohgosh-buttons.com

Tangible Light Studio
Woodland Hills, CA 91364
(858) 232-8276
tangible-light.com

The Spirited Bead & Klew's Gallery
435 W. J St.
Tehachapi, CA 93561
(661) 823-1930
klewexpressions.com

TOOLS

Wubbers Bail-Making Pliers
Jewels By Jules
(520) 419-4183
jewels-by-jules.com

Index

Arched Loop, 16

beads, adding, 28

Cloverleaf, 20–21; Five-Loop Cloverleaf, 21; Straight Three-Loop Cloverleaf, 21; Three-Loop Cloverleaf, 20

ear wires, 27
Elegant Elle, 22; Elegant Elle Eye, 27; Elegant Elle Hook, 26

Five-Loop Cloverleaf, 21
flush cut, 14
flush cutters, 9, 14

Heart, 23

jump rings, 18–19; cutting, 19; making, 18; opening/closing, 19; sizes, 18

liver of sulfur (LOS), 11, 30
loops, 14–17; Arched Loop, 16; P-Shaped Loop, 14–15; Regal Loop, 17; with round-nose pliers, 14; Simple Loop, 15; sizing, 13; Wrapped Loop, 16–17

mandrels, 10, 14; bracelet mandrel, 10; measuring and marking for loops, 14; ring mandrel, 10

P-Shaped Loop, 14–15

pinch cut, 14
pliers: bail-making, 9, 13, 18; chain-nose, 9, 13; flat-nose, 9, 13; holding, 12; matching to wire, 13; nylon-jaw bracelet-forming, 10; nylon-jaw wire-straightening, 10, 13; rolling, 13

Regal Loop, 17
Regal Scroll, 24
Regal Shape, 25

Scroll, 23
Shepherd's Hook, 25
Silver Black, 11, 30
Simple Loop, 15
Straight Three-Loop Cloverleaf, 21

taping shapes together, 25
Three-Loop Cloverleaf, 20

wire, 6–8; aligning, 13; choosing, 7; cleaning, 8; coiling, 28; controlling, 12; copper, 6; craft, 6; dead-soft, 7; filing ends, 30; flexibility, 12; gauge, 6; half-hard, 7; half-round, 7; hard, 7; hardness, 7; holding, 12; oxidizing, 30; recycling, 8; round, 7; shaping, 20–27; spring-back, 7; square, 7; stability, 12; sterling silver, 6; storing, 8; straightening, 8; weaving, 29
Wrapped Loop, 16–17

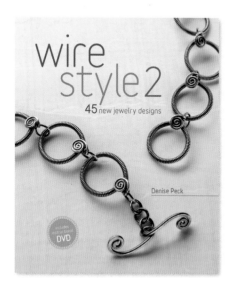
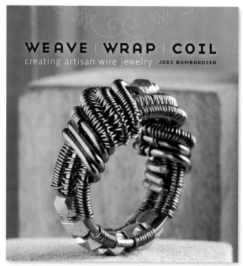
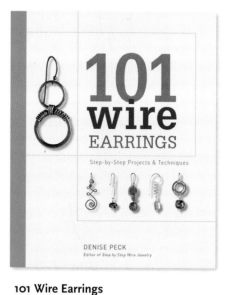